44.00

ROUND THE YEAR
WITH THE
WORLD'S RELIGIONS

DANCING ROUND THE MAY-POLE IN THE DAYS OF CHAUCER
(From an old print)

ROUND THE YEAR
WITH THE
WORLD'S RELIGIONS

by

ROYSTON PIKE

With four Plates in Colour,
and many Drawings by
E. C. MANSELL

Henry Schuman   New York

Republished by Omnigraphics ● Penobscot Building ● Detroit ● 1993

PUBLISHED 1950, BY HENRY SCHUMAN, INC.,
20 EAST 70TH STREET, NEW YORK 21, N.Y.

Library of Congress Cataloging-in-Publication Data

Pike, Royston, 1896–
    Round the year with the world's religions / by Royston Pike.
        p.   cm.
    Originally published: New York : Henry Schuman, 1950.
    Includes index.
    ISBN 1-55888-996-5 (lib. bdg. : acid-free paper)
    1. Festivals.   2. Fasts and feasts.   I. Title.
GT3932.P55   1993
394.2'65—dc20   93-24134
                                                               CIP

Printed in the United States of America

CONTENTS

LIST OF PLATES

JANUARY

AGES and ages ago, the world was a very much nicer place to live in than it is now. It was indeed the happiest time that has ever been, and those who were born then were very fortunate. Always a boy and a girl were born together—twins, so that they were never lonely. It is true that when each pair of twins was forty-nine days old their parents died, but in those days children had small appetites —a grain of corn was enough for dinner ; and besides, with every pair of twins grew up ten marvellous trees, which supplied them with all that they could possibly want.

Thus one tree produced the most delicious fruits, so sweet that there was no need for sugar ; another gave a bright light that shone all through the night, and a third looked like a Christmas-tree covered with fairy-lamps ; the leaves of the fourth made sweet music as they rustled in the wind, and out of the leaves of the fifth were formed little pots and pans ; the flowers of the sixth were exquisitely shaped and gave off a most lovely scent ; the seventh gave food that was beyond complaint, and the eighth's leaves were shaped so beautifully that they served as jewels. As for the last two, one provided just enough clothes to wear in a climate that was always warm, and the other was a house, a palace rather, ready furnished to live in. The children had everything that they could wish for, and when they were fully grown the man was six miles high, and the woman not much shorter. Moreover, they had two hundred and fifty-six ribs each. They were good, too; they never killed anything, whether in sport or for food or in quarrels or war. Nor did they ever eat cooked food, for that in those days was thought to be as grave a sin as murdering the man next door.

But that good time was too good to last. After millions of years it was followed by a period that was only half as happy. The twins did not live for anything like so long, had only one hundred and twenty-eight ribs, and were only four miles high when fully grown. They had to eat rather more, and they got hungry oftener. But each boy and girl was still provided with a complete collection of wonderful trees.

This period also came to an end, and in the next age the twins were only two miles high, had sixty-four ribs, and lived only half as long. Nor were they always happy: a little care, a little sorrow, crept into their lives. Perhaps, too, it was not altogether an advantage that in this age there was born a girl who when she grew up invented eighteen different alphabets, and so made learning much more difficult, since there was so much more to learn.

In the next age the men and women were not much more than a hundred yards in height, their ribs numbered thirty-two, and they got so hungry that they had to eat a good meal every day; the man had thirty-two morsels of food at a sitting, and a woman twenty-eight. This period too passed, and there dawned an age that was by comparison the worst yet. No man could expect to live beyond

2

a hundred and twenty-five years, or to be more than ten feet high, or to have more than sixteen ribs. This period is the one in which we are living at the present time (but actually we have twenty-four ribs !). We have only to read the newspapers to realize that for great numbers of people in all parts of the world it is a very bad time in which to be alive. But things might be worse. And they will be worse. After twenty-one thousand years this bad age will come to an end and be followed by an age very much more unpleasant, in which a man will be old at sixteen or twenty, will have only eight ribs, and never be more than eighteen inches tall.

And what a world he will find himself in ! The days will be terribly hot and the nights terribly cold, and disease and sickness will keep the doctors ever so busy. Then there will come great tempests ; and before the tremendous gales, men and animals, even the trees and plants, will try to find a hiding-place away from it all, in caves and in the depths of the sea. But the awful time will pass, and slowly, ever so slowly, things will get a little better, men will grow a little taller, and they will have a few more ribs.*

Such is the belief of the Jains, one of the peoples of India. There are not many of them, comparatively speaking : only a million and a half, compared with the three hundred millions of India as a whole ; and they and their religion are on the decline. We shall meet them again later on in this little book, but I have quoted this belief of theirs in

* See Mrs. Sinclair Stevenson, *The Heart of Jainism* (Oxford University Press).

Avasarpini, a time that is getting gradually worse, and Utsarpini, a time that is gradually getting better, as typical of what is held by many of the world's peoples—that time is like a wheel that keeps on turning and turning, now for the better and now for the worse. The Jains think that it is a good serpent who is responsible for the upward push and a bad serpent for the downward drag. But that is just their guess, their " shot " at explaining what is surely about the most difficult thing in the world to explain—Time. (" Space " is about as difficult.)

When we try to imagine a time before Time had begun, we just cannot do it. Nor can we have any idea of what would happen if Time should come to an end. We just have to take the idea as we find it, and try to make do with the dictionary definition of time as " duration : continued existence." Then the sun comes to our assistance. It rises and sets, so there is what we call day and night; the world moves round it, and in 365 days (more or less) arrives back at (more or less) where it started from. The moon, too, gives a hand, and by measuring the period between one full moon and the next we have roughly speaking a month. Days, months, years. . . . These are like the markings on a ruler. They make it possible for us to note how " time is passing " —*Tempus fugit*, as the Latin inscription runs on the sundials that one sometimes finds in old gardens.

Janus the Two-faced

So here we are, in this particular instant of Time, looking back on an immensely long past and looking forward to—who knows ?—an immensely long future.

4

From our point we are facing both ways, just as did Janus, the old Roman god after whom January, the first month in the year, is named. His image was two-faced, and it was said that this was because of his wisdom : he knew the past and he knew the future too. Another view is that it was supposed to indicate his constant vigilance and wakefulness : he was always looking both before and behind, and it was probably because of this idea that a little bust of Janus was placed near the front door of Roman houses, where he could keep an eye—or rather two eyes —on what was going on. The Latin word for a door is *janua*, and some scholars have asserted that it comes from Janus, the god who kept the door or gate. Whether this be so or not, Janus was regarded as the god who opens things and fastens them up, and he developed into the god of beginnings : he was the god of the first hour of the day and, as we have just seen, of the first month in the year.

JANUS, ON AN OLD ROMAN COIN

When, in the great days of the Roman Empire, Rome was the capital of the world (or so its people liked to think), there was a famous shrine bearing Janus's name standing in the Forum, the chief square or market-place. It does not appear to have been a very large or imposing building, but it was remarkable for its bronze doors on the western and

5

eastern sides that stood open in time of war and were closed in time of peace. The famous Latin poet Virgil refers to them in a passage in his *Aeneid*. " A solemn custom was observed of old," he writes —I am using the translation made by the seventeenth-century English poet John Dryden—" which now the Romans hold. . . ."

> Two gates of steel (the name of Mars they bear,
> And still are worshipped with religious fear)
> Before his temple stand : the dire abode,
> And the feared issues of the furious god,
> Are fenced with brazen bolts ; without the gates,
> The wary guardian Janus doubly waits.
> Then when the sacred senate votes the wars,
> The Roman consul their decree declares,
> And in his robes the sounding gates unbars.
> The youth in military shouts arise,
> And the loud trumpets break the yielding skies.

As everyone knows, the Romans were a very war-like people, so that it is hardly surprising to learn that the doors of Janus's temple were closed only twice in the seven hundred years that preceded the establishment of the Empire under Augustus, Julius Caesar's grand-nephew. Augustus, who was not particularly fond of fighting, has left it on record that in his forty years' reign the gates were shut three times, and in the reigns of later emperors they were closed for many years at a time.

Welcoming the New Year

January 1 was New Year's Day with the ancient Romans as it is with us, and they used to give one another presents ; one of the emperors made it a rule that no one could *demand* a present except on this day—a provision that the children no doubt took

6

full advantage of. In England in olden days New Year's Eve and New Year's Day were a time of merry-making, of feasting and good cheer. In castle and cottage the father used to gather his family and friends around a bowl of ale spiced with cloves, nutmeg, and ginger, all piping hot, from which he drank their healths, and then each in turn drank from the bowl as it was passed round. " Waes hael ! " they said, these being the Anglo-Saxon words for " May you be in good health ! " or " Here's to you ! ", as we might say. So the bowl came to be known as the Wassail, and the

A WASSAIL BOWL

general jollification was called wassailing. Sometimes the poorer folk decorated a bowl with ribbons and took it round from door to door begging for a coin or two to put in it, so that they might enjoy the good things of life besides the rich. Children in particular were fond of this old custom, and they used to sing :

> We are not daily beggars
>   That beg from door to door ;
> But we are neighbours' children,
>   Whom you have seen before.
>
> We have got a little purse,
>   Made of stretching leather skin,
> We want a little of your money
>   To line it well within.
>
> Bring us out a table
>   And spread it with a cloth ;
> Bring us out a mouldy cheese,
>   And some of your Christmas loaf.

7

God bless the master of this house,
Likewise the mistress too,
And all the little children,
That round the table go !

In Scotland—where New Year's Day is " kept up "
much more than it is in England : indeed, it is a
Bank Holiday—there was another old custom called
the " first foot." Just before midnight on the last
day of the old year, the grown-ups (the children
were supposed to be tucked up in bed and fast
asleep, of course) sallied out, carrying a kettle of
hot drink and a good supply of buns and shortbread,
or bread and cheese, and visited their friends' houses.
If they were the first to enter the door since midnight
—if, that is, they were the first visitors of the New
Year—then they received a particularly hearty welcome because they were supposed to bring good
luck with them. The kettle was quickly emptied,
and the buns and cakes were shared by one and all.

Among the younger folk there was a special kind
of " first foot." The young men used to knock at
the door in the hope that it would be opened by
their sweetheart ; but sometimes, we are told, it
was jokingly arranged that not pretty Jenny but the
oldest lady in the house should be sent to " see
who's there " and obtain the expected kiss.

Coming soon after New Year's Day, if it did not
happen to be New Year's Day itself, was another
old Scottish festival—the first Monday in January,
that was called Handsel Monday (" Handsel " is
from the Anglo-Saxon word meaning " something
given into the hands of another "), when the equivalent of Christmas-boxes were given to postmen,

8

dustmen and roadsweepers, and newspaper-boys. On that day, too, boys and girls might expect " tips " from their parents, or as often perhaps from their aunts and uncles ; while farmers were in the habit of inviting all their servants and labourers to a really substantial breakfast of beef and bacon, washed down by plenty of ale and not a little whisky.

Joys of the Twelfth Night

Talking of gifts brings us naturally enough to Twelfth Day, that is, January 6, the twelfth day after Christmas. In the Church calendar this is the festival of the Epiphany—the word comes from the Greek for " appearance "—which commemorates the appearance or manifestation to the Gentiles (that is, those who are not Jews) of Jesus Christ as a babe in the manger at Bethlehem. To the humble cradle, so runs the story given in St. Matthew's Gospel in the New Testament, were led by a star three Magi, or Wise Men of the East ; and before it they fell down and worshipped, and gave of their treasures of gold and spices. Many a later story has gathered about the three visitors ; they have been given names, and are said to have been kings, and to lie buried in the cathedral of Cologne, in the German Rhineland. In the Middle Ages it was customary at this time of year to perform in the village church or town hall a little play or drama, whose subject was the visit of the Wise Men to Bethlehem. Indeed, Twelfth Night, the eve of Twelfth Day, was for long a very popular festival both with the poor and lowly and the rich and powerful.

While no doubt the chief reason was to do honour to the Three Kings or Wise Men, there are grounds for believing that the joyous celebration is older than Christianity. Thus there was one old custom called the " election of the Kings by beans " that may have been derived from a game played by Roman children in ancient times at this season of the year. The Roman boys and girls drew lots with beans to decide who among them should act as their king in play-time ; in England and France and other countries of Western Europe in the Middle Ages mothers used to make a big cake in which a bean was inserted (very much as today a threepenny-bit is slipped into the Christmas pudding). When all the family had sat down to dinner, the cake was divided by lot, and whoever got the piece containing the bean was called " King of the Bean." For that day he was accepted as " King," even though he were the youngest there, and everything that he said was supposed to be law.

Sir James Frazer, a great scholar who wrote a series of books called *The Golden Bough* * that are filled with stories of the strangest beliefs and customs, suggested that the King of the Bean (like the Abbot of Unreason, the Lord of Misrule, and other similar personages whom we may read about in Sir Walter Scott's and other historical novels) may have been the successors of the real man who, in the early days of the Roman state, impersonated the god Saturn in the revels that were held at the end of December—and, when the revels were over, was slain as a sacrifice. Be this as it may, it is true enough that this period

* Published by Macmillan & Co., Ltd.

when December joins January is one that is marked with ceremonies of one kind or another in many parts of the world. If we ask the reason, then it is because the period follows the winter solstice (a word that comes from the Latin for " sun " and " stand "), when the sun seems to stop going ever farther and farther away, and stands still for a while before starting on its return journey, bringing with it first the springtime and then the summer. So it is only natural that men should rejoice. (Try to imagine what would happen if the sun kept on going away, and never came back. Our primitive ancestors were not so sure as we are that " he " would not forget to turn at the right time !)

Gift-day in India

To take a case in point, in India, about the time of Twelfth Night with us, there is celebrated a very happy festival known as Sankranti. This marks the beginning of a new day for the gods, with whom a day and a night are supposed each to last six months. The gods' night begins in the middle of July, and then for six months they are asleep, and the evil spirits or demons take advantage of the opportunity to creep out of their lairs and see what harm they can do among men. But on Sankranti the gods wake up, and to celebrate the occasion the Hindus make it a day of almsgiving. Green chick-peas are picked and podded, and placed in black earthenware pots, and these are given, with sesamum seeds and some articles of clothing, to the best of the Brahmans—the gentlemen of the highest caste, or, if there is none of these available, then to the first beggar who is encountered in the street. Sometimes the Brahmans and Sadhus (holy beggars) do not wait to be met, but go out to meet the gift-bringers. In return they promise that all who give them alms will live happily, if not for ever after, at least for all the coming year. On Sankranti women make presents to their " in-laws "—practically every woman in India is married or is a widow ; sisters-in-law in particular may expect to receive a pound of clarified butter and a pound of sugar.

Nor are the animals forgotten. The villagers collect all the cows, and the men offer them fresh hay, while the women give them sweets and paint their foreheads with the yellow colouring obtained from saffron leaves.

This day is also held to be specially lucky for betrothals or engagements. A girl whose turn it is to be married in the coming year does her hair with particular care, takes a cold bath early in the morning, and then carries the water in a pot to her fiancé's home, where it is thrown away just as she sits down to the family meal.

Returning to the England of our great-grandfathers, the day after Twelfth Day—that is, January 7 —was known jokingly as St. Distaff's Day, because it was then that the women of the household began to use again their distaff (stick for holding the wool or flax, etc., in spinning) after the twelve days' break since Christmas. (That spinning was the recognized occupation of unmarried ladies is shown by our word " spinster ".) As the girls got out their distaffs and fixed them in position on the spinning-wheels, the jolly young ploughboys would put a light to the flax; whereupon the girls would retaliate by pouring buckets of water over their tormentors.

Then the first Monday after Twelfth Day was Plough Monday, which like Distaff Day was the occasion for a final fling of fun and games before the hard work of winter was taken up again. In country districts the ploughmen used to dress up

PLOUGH MONDAY REVELS (*from an old print*)

a plough with bright-coloured ribbons and drag it round the parish, stopping at each house in turn and demanding a gift. If a farmer, obviously well off, refused to give a present, the ploughshare was driven across the patch of garden in front of his door so as to make it as rough as a newly-ploughed field. Probably none of the ploughboys knew the why and wherefore of the strange proceeding, but it is supposed that in the centuries when England

13

was a Catholic land the ploughmen used to burn candles in front of certain saints' images in the parish church with a view to obtaining their blessing, and the annual procession was intended to provide the funds for buying the " plough lights," as they were called. At the Reformation the candles were put out and never lit again, but the processions, being jolly affairs and profitable enough (to the ploughmen at least), were kept up until almost our own day.

Still turning the leaves of January on the calendar, we come to the 14th, on which was formerly celebrated the Feast of the Ass, in memory of the flight of Joseph and Mary with the Infant Jesus into Egypt, when they had been warned that King Herod intended to kill the Child. As with the incident of the Wise Men at Epiphany, there used to be a dramatic performance that was intended to bring home the story to those—they were the great majority—who had no Bibles, and would not have been able to read them if they had. A beautiful girl, holding a baby to her breast, was seated on a gaily-harnessed ass and led through the streets in solemn procession. Having arrived at the church, they entered—ass and all—and there was a service in which the people, instead of making the usual responses, brayed irreverently like an ass.

St. Agnes's Eve

Another week goes by, and we come to St. Agnes's Day (January 21). Agnes, we are told, was a young Roman maiden who because she was a Christian suffered the most horrible tortures and was at length put to death. That was about A.D. 304, and to this day a religious procession is held in Rome every year on her " day." Agnes was unmarried, and this was no doubt the chief reason that led young girls to seek her assistance in the discovery of their future husbands. Certain it is that until not so very long ago—indeed, it may still continue in some country districts—it was the custom for maidens to practise some strange tricks. There is a famous poem by John Keats called " The Eve of Saint Agnes," which runs :

> They told her how, upon St. Agnes's Eve,
> Young virgins might have visions of delight,
> And soft adorings from their loves receive
> Upon the honey'd middle of the night,
> If ceremonies due they did aright;
> As, supperless to bed they must retire,
> And couch supine their beauties, lily white;
> Nor look behind, nor sideways, but require
> Of Heaven with upward eyes for all that they desire.

In the poem all goes well : Madeleine and the man she is to marry escape together from the castle in which she has been imprisoned. But there is a similar story told by George Borrow in that strangely-named but fascinating book of English travel, *Lavengro*, that has a very different ending.

The Wake of Freya

Young George, it is quite clear, was a " bit of a problem" to his parents and to his schoolmasters. The only thing he seemed to be really good at was learning out-of-the-way languages, including the gipsy speech. One evening his father—an old retired soldier—and his mother were discussing his future, and Mrs. Borrow gave as an instance of the boy's extraordinary knowledge his interpretation of a very weird experience that she had had as a girl.

A superstition lies at the bottom of it, as old as the Danes. So at least says the child, who by some means or other has of late become acquainted with their language. He says that the Danes were once a mighty people, and were masters of the land where we at present are; that they had gods of their own, strange and wild like themselves, and that it was their god Frey who gave his name to what we call Friday. This Frey had a wife whose name was Freya, and the child says that the old pagans considered them as the gods of love and marriage, and worshipped them as such; and that all young damsels were in the habit of addressing themselves to Freya in their love adventures, and of requesting her assistance. He told me, and he quite frightened me when he said it, that a certain night ceremony, in which I took part in my early youth, was neither more nor less than an invocation to this Freya, the wife of the old pagan god.

Then as they sit in the garden in the deepening dusk Mrs. Borrow describes how, when she was a girl of ten, a considerably older sister had a great desire to know whether she was to be married or not. " So she determined upon the wake, the night-watch of Freya, as the child calls it." The two girls went into town and bought a fine linen handkerchief, which they washed in the running water of a brook on the way home. Then, sitting together in the kitchen, as eleven struck they hung up the hand-kerchief to dry before the fire, and set the door just a little ajar. Shivering with cold and fear, and not speaking a word, they awaited the footsteps of the man who was to become the girl's husband. Suddenly as the clock struck three the gate slammed. With a shriek the elder sister banged and bolted the door, and just as she went into hysterics, they both thought that they heard something moaning at the door. . . .

The girl was ill for many weeks, and when she recovered, made a poor marriage and was never happy. Mrs. Borrow said that the incident happened on a wild December night, and the prayer was offered to no Christian saint but to a heathen goddess. Yet there can be little doubt that here, as in the case of many another religious festival, there has been a mingling of Christian story with the superstitions that our pagan ancestors believed in when they came in their long-boats to raid and pillage and eventually settle in what was not yet called England.

FEBRUARY

IF we had been in Rome on a certain day in 44 B.C.; if we had mixed with the carpenters and cobblers and other " mechanicals " who crowded the pavements, we should have seen what they had come to see—a number of men dressed in goatskins running as hard as they could go along the streets that lay round the Palatine Hill; and as they rushed past, lashing at the people with strips of goatskin as narrow and cutting as a whip. And, stranger still, those in their way made no attempt to get out of it. On the contrary, they thrust themselves in front of the runners, and women in particular—highly respectable, well-dressed, gentle women—danced with glee when the heavy thongs cut them across the body.

If we had asked who were the runners, we should have been told that most of them were holy men, priests in the service of the god Lupercus, but one of them was none other than Mark Antony, the eminent statesman.

That celebration of the Lupercalia, as the performance was called, lives in history since Mark Antony, in the course of his wild progress, rushed up the steps of the Rostra or platform and offered Julius Caesar the crown (which, as is told in Shakespeare's play, he refused). But the race through the Roman streets was an annual occurrence, and it continued to be run for a hundred and fifty years after Christianity had become the official faith.

18

Not very much is known about Lupercus; he may have been the same as the woodland god called Faunus, whom some of the Roman scholars made out was the Greek god Pan. But whoever he was, his worshippers believed that he was a powerful god whose favour was well worth the obtaining; and they believed, too, that those who were whipped in the mad race through the Roman streets were cleansed of their sins and were sure to be very fortunate in the year that lay ahead. Thus any woman who received a whipping would become the mother of a bonny baby.

A strange custom indeed, and strange to learn that to it we owe the name of the second month in our year. For the thongs that the runners made to whistle through the air and wielded so vigorously were called in Latin *februa*, that is, " means of purification " ; whence *Februarius* and our February.

St. Valentine's Day

The actual day of the Lupercalia was February 15, and the ceremony seems to have been held not only in Rome but in some other Italian cities. Associated with it was a variety of other ceremonies, and one of these (we are told) consisted of the placing of slips of parchment bearing the names of young women into a box, whence they were drawn by eligible young men. When the Christian Church began to grow in numbers and influence its leaders did what they could to make conversion easy by adopting in a modified form as many as possible of the old pagan customs. In this instance they substituted on the slips of parchment the names of saints for the names of the young girls; and as St. Valentine, a Christian bishop in Rome who had been martyred in the third century, was supposed to have been beheaded about the middle of February, they tried to get the people to observe his festival in place of that of the Lupercalia. Such at least is one explanation that has been given of the origin of St. Valentine's Day—which is, however, February 14.

No more is known about the Christian saint than about the Roman god. Certainly there is no clear connection between him and the custom of sending "Valentines." Nowadays these are anonymous letters, and often if not always they are intended to be humorous. But up to the eighteenth century there was a ceremony on Valentine's Eve that was a lottery very like the one which is said to have been held in ancient Rome in connection with the Lupercalia.

The young folk in England and Scotland, says an old traveller, followed a very ancient custom. An equal number of girls and young bachelors got together, and each wrote their name on a piece of paper, which they rolled up and put in a hat. Then they had a draw, and the young man drawn by a girl was called her Valentine. It was expected of the Valentines that they should take their ladies to a party, and often what had begun as a simple game developed into a love that was true and lasting.

In Samuel Pepy's famous *Diary* there are several references to the old practice of "drawing a Valentine." Thus on St. Valentine's Day in 1667 he writes, "This morning come up to my wife's bedside, I being dressing myself, little Will Mercer to be her Valentine; and brought her name writ on blue paper in gold letters, done by himself, very pretty; and we were both well pleased with it. But I am also this year my wife's Valentine, and it will cost me £5; but that I must have laid out if we had not been Valentines." A day or two later he remarks on the custom of drawing mottoes as well as names, and that his wife's is " Most courteous and most fair," which he thinks " very pretty."

" Hail to thy returning festival, old Bishop Valentine ! " writes Charles Lamb in one of his *Essays of Elia.* " Immortal Go-between ; who and what manner of person art thou ? Art thou but a *name*, typifying the restless principle which impels poor humans to seek perfection in union ? or wert thou indeed a mortal prelate with thy apron on, and lawn sleeves ? " Not all Valentines are foolish, he goes on to say, and tells of a kind friend of his, an artist, who sent a delightfully drawn and painted Valentine to a young girl who lived opposite and who by her kindly smile had often brought a touch of gladness into his heart. " She was all joyousness and innocence, and just of an age to enjoy receiving a Valentine " ; and peeping across the road from behind his window-curtain " he saw, unseen, the happy girl unfold the Valentine, dance about, clap her hands as one after the other the pretty emblems unfolded themselves." She had no lover ; or if she had, none she knew that could have created the bright pictures that so delighted her. So the Valentine came like some fairy present or as " a Godsend, as our familiarly pious ancestors termed a benefit received where the benefactor was unknown. It

21

would do her no harm. It would do her good for
ever after."

Devil-Dancers in Tibet

Just about the time—in some years, at least—that
young people here at home are dropping into the
pillar-boxes the Cupid-decorated and anonymous
missives, away in the heart of Asia, high up in the
mountains of the " roof of the world," the Tibetans
are celebrating their New Year festival. They are
a highly religious people, professing a form of the
Buddhist faith ; theirs is the only country in the
world in which nearly all the power is exercised by
priests and monks. The head of the State and also
of the Church is the Dalai Lama, a great official
who is supposed to be a reincarnation of Chenrezi,
the " Lord of Mercy " who is the patron deity of
the country.

Another very out-of-the-ordinary thing in Tibet
is the calendar. The year-names are made up of
one of five elements, viz. earth, iron, water, wood,
and fire, joined with the male or female of one of
twelve animals—dog, pig, ox, tiger, hare, dragon,
serpent, horse, sheep, monkey, mouse, and bird.
Thus one year may be named wood male mouse or
wood female bull, fire male tiger, earth female dragon,
and so on. These are arranged in cycles or series, a
new cycle beginning at the end of every sixtieth year.

New Year's Day is the greatest festival in the
Tibetan year, and it is made the occasion for weird
and wonderful performances. Not many Europeans
have ever had the opportunity of witnessing them,
and among the few have been Sir Charles Bell, who

represented Britain in Tibet and the adjacent countries, and Mr. Spencer Chapman, who has made expeditions to the Arctic and climbed mountains in the Himalayas, partly for the fun of it and partly for some scientific reason, such as the collection of flowers and plants that are very rare or even unknown to our botanists.

To make sure of having a Happy New Year the Tibetans think it essential that all the bad influences that have spoiled so much of the old year shall be cast out. The way they do this is by a " Devil Dance " that takes place just before the end of the old year, in one of the courtyards of the vast palace in Lhasa—the capital of Tibet—known as the Potala. The scene is startling in its liveliness, in the bright colours of the silken robes worn by the monk-officials and the people who have come to see the show. First to perform are the soldiers, who are wearing bits and pieces of ancient armour, plumed head-dresses, and shields of basket-work. They dance the war-dance, pretend to engage in fierce combat, chant their battle-hymns and shout their war-cries, then wind up with a tremendous bang as they discharge their antiquated guns. When the smoke has cleared away, a band plays a selection of Tibetan music with trumpets and drums and gongs. Then the " devil-dancers " make their appearance : monks dressed in gorgeous robes and wearing huge masks—some with horns to represent bulls and stags, some with greatly magnified human faces painted hideously in gold and scarlet and green, with bulging eyes and great fangs where teeth should be. After much hopping and twisting and

turning, these make way for the " skeleton dancers "
whose masks are skeleton heads, whose black robes
are painted with grey bones, whose fingers are horrible claws. Finally there may be the Black Hat
dancers, who wear immense pyramidal hats made of
wood and crowned by little skulls and bunches of
peacock feathers.

Slowly the dancers move round and round their

DEVIL DANCERS IN TIBET

leader, the " Chief of the Wizards," who stands in
the middle of the stage, weaving spells. So they
go on for hours and hours until the master magician
pours some spirit into a huge cauldron of oil that
is bubbling and boiling over a fire of crackling
thorns. There is a flash of flame. Burning oil
runs over the floor, and at the same time a piece of
paper on which are painted a number of black

devils is flung into the fire. This is the end. The devils have been defeated, thrust out, destroyed. The New Year may now arrive in perfect safety.

The next few days are marked by a variety of shows, processions, archery competitions, and the like. Formerly the chief attraction was the sight of men sliding down long ropes of yak-hair stretching from the battlements of the Potala to a stone pillar hundreds of feet below. The men sat on leather saddles, but even so they were generally more or less severely injured when they had shot down the rope. At last one was nearly killed, and the Dalai Lama ordered that some other less dangerous acrobatic feat must be substituted in future. So now a man is hauled to the top of a fifty-foot-high pole, where he swings himself round and round on a metal post.

In the last few days of the festival the city is filled with monks, or lamas—a large part of the Tibetan population are lamas, i.e. men who are not usually married, and who live perhaps not very useful lives in huge monasteries—twenty thousand or perhaps thirty thousand of them. Every day religious services are held in the chief church or cathedral, the Jo-Kang, which was built thirteen hundred years ago to house Buddhist images that had been brought to Tibet by King Song-tsen Gam-po's two new wives, one of whom came from Nepal and the other from China. Crown of everything is the Great Prayer Festival, lasting for three weeks in February and March, whose object is the speeding on his way of the next Buddha. For though we usually speak of Buddha as if there had been only one, Gautama Buddha, who lived some 500 years before Christ, the Buddhists of Tibet and many other lands hold that there has been a long succession of these " enlightened ones." The Buddha who is to come will be the Buddha of Conquering Love ; and when he comes, the world, so it is believed, will be a much better and happier place.

New Year in China

With the Chinese, too, the New Year usually begins some time in our February, and many a queer custom is associated with it, although what with the long succession of wars that for so many years have made the lives of the Chinese millions miserable, it may be doubted whether some of these customs are still performed—at any rate on the same scale as of old. One of them consisted of a sacrifice to a spirit known as the Divine Husbandman, who was represented as having a bull's head on a man's body. The sacrifice was a make-believe one, consisting of a large effigy or figure of an ox, cow, or buffalo made out of coloured bits of paper pasted on a wooden frame, and filled with different sorts of grain. The colours were supposed to give some indication of what the coming year would be like ; thus, if there was much red, then there would be many fires, or if white predominated, then floods and rain might be expected. The effigy was placed just outside the east gate of the city or town, and then the governor of the place walked in solemn procession round it, accompanied by the leading mandarins (officials and scholars). As they did so, they beat at the figure with slender rods, and the grain poured out from the holes they made. When it was quite broken up, the figure was set on fire, and there followed a scramble among the spectators for the pieces of charred paper, since these were believed to be very lucky. Finally, a real ox was killed, and the meat was divided among the mandarins. It should be added that in China, New Year's Day is the first day of spring, and the custom that has just been described is an example of a kind of springtime magic that is performed in many parts of the world.

Burning the Witch in India

Spring comes early, too, in India, towards the end of February and in early March, and then it is that the Hindus celebrate the festival of Holi. This lasts for three days, and at the bottom of it is a story, a kind of not very pleasant fairy tale, about a wicked old witch who came to a bad end. Here is the story, as told in a book called *The Rites of the Twice-born* * by Mrs. Sinclair Stevenson, who was a Christian missionary in Gujarat, in North-West India. (The "Twice-born," by the way, are the members of the higher castes, who are "born" for a second time when they—the boys at least—are invested with the sacred cord or thread, which they wear henceforth as a sign of caste membership.)

Once upon a time there was a demon called Hiranya-kasipu, who had a pious son called Prahlada. Unfortunately the two did not hit it off, for, if the father was a demon, the son was a prig, and, irritated by the son's appalling self-righteousness, the father tried to kill him in all sorts of ways. But neither poisoning nor drowning proved successful, and at last the demon-father persuaded his witch-sister (and a very bad witch she was, too) called

* Published by the Oxford University Press.

Holika, to take her impeccable nephew on her lap. The father thought that, whatever he did, nothing would ever hurt his sister—she was so very wicked—so he promised that she should escape unscathed, and promptly set fire to both aunt and nephew. However, the virtue of the youth saved him, and the aunt it was who died, burned to death in the most horrible manner.

That is one version of the story that explains the Holi festival; but in the villages, Mrs. Sinclair Stevenson goes on to say, an even more thrilling story was told her to account for the Holi fire. Once upon a time there was a witch of the name of Holika, who made herself such a nuisance that at last the people burnt her in a fire of cow-dung cakes. (In India, where wood and coal are scarce, cow dung is the ordinary fuel.) So that no other witches should hear her shrieks and rush to save her, all the men and the children round the fire shouted so as to drown her cries. At the same time they were so cruel as to pelt her with coconuts. Then just before she died they thought that as an evil spirit she might do more harm to them dead than she had been able to do when alive, so they threw to her in the fire some dates and handfuls of fried beans, and offered her a drink of milk.

So much for the story; now for the festival. On the first day the children in town and village go from house to house, beating drums, singing rude songs, and generally making a nuisance of themselves. From each house they beg cakes of grain and cow dung, which they pile in a heap above a hole in which has been buried an earthenware pot filled with water and grain or peas and beans. Round the pile the children hang garlands of cow-dung cakes, to make it quite plain to everyone that it is supposed to represent the horrid old witch. The next day is Holi Day itself, and the people give each other presents of tit-bits from their food cupboards. Then a light is applied to the pile, and as the bonfire blazes the men and women and little children walk slowly round it three, four, or seven times, and throw into the flames dates and coconuts. At the same time they sing and say all the nastiest things that they can think of, just to show their detestation of the horrid old witch. As soon as the fire has died down, there is a rush to dig up the buried pot. If all the grain inside is well cooked, then it is assumed that there will be no fear of famine in the coming year; but if the grain on one side only is properly baked, then the fields facing that side will have bountiful harvests, while those on the opposite side will be stricken with famine. If none of the grain is cooked—that hardly bears thinking of, since it is a sign that throughout the length and breadth of the land the crops will fail and there will be famine, starvation, and death.

Now the grown-ups go home and eat the nicest cakes that they have been able to make, but the girls of the village have still something important to do. First they pour water over the ashes of the bonfire. Some of these they spread in a circle, and with the rest they make a little image of Parvati, one of the most important goddesses whom Hindus love to worship. This strange doll they decorate with garlands of cotton-wool and daub with bright colours; then they put it in the middle of the circle, scatter grain over it, and knock their knuckles against its head. In so doing they pretend to take all the troubles of the goddess on their own shoulders, and they wind up the proceedings by saying their prayers to Parvati. On fifteen days in succession they repeat their worship, and it is generally believed that their reverence will be rewarded in the shape of a handsome young husband.

A Bed for Bridget

A strange custom indeed; yet there is no need to go so far to find customs nearly if not quite as strange. In northern lands February is at the turn of the seasons, when the long winter sleep is just beginning to be broken, and trees and plants show signs of the near approach of spring. What more natural, then, that simple country folk should feel themselves called upon to do all in their power to hasten the return of the sun, bringing with him warmth and light and the promise and prospect of good crops and increased flocks and herds? This would seem to be the reason for a curious custom of the people of the Hebrides Islands, off the west coast of Scotland, associated with February 1, or Candlemas Eve. In the Church calendar Candlemas (February 2) commemorates the presentation of the infant Jesus in the Temple at Jerusalem, and its name comes from the ceremony of blessing candles and carrying them in procession on that day, as a reminder that Christ came as a Light into the world. But the custom in question has nothing to do with Christianity. The mistress and servants of each family used to take a sheaf of oats, dress it up in women's clothes, put it in a large basket, and lay a wooden club beside it. This they called " Briid's bed," and then the mistress and the servants cried three times " Briid is come, Briid is welcome ! " This they did just before going to bed, and as soon as they got up in the morning they made a most careful examination of the ashes on the hearth, hoping to see there the mark of Briid's club ; if they did, then they took it as an exceedingly good omen, and if they could find no trace, then they would be unlucky indeed. Another old writer says that on the night before Candlemas it was usual to make a bed with corn and hay, over which some blankets were laid, in a part of the house near the door. When all was ready, one of the family went outside and called several times, " Bridget, Bridget, come in ; thy bed is ready ! " Candles were left burning beside the bed all night.

Who Briid was, we do not know. There are several Brides and Bridgets among the Christian saints, and February 1 is the " day " of the Irish St. Bride or St. Bridget, who was a Christian princess of Ulster ; but it is not at all clear why beds should be made for them in Scottish homesteads and in the Isle of Man, where a very similar custom was once to be found. So it is now thought that long before Christianity came to these islands, there was among the Celts or " ancient Britons " a goddess named Brigit, who was the goddess of fire and also, it would seem, of fertility of the crops and of men.

MARCH

IT was a beautiful day in early spring, and in the warm sunshine Persephone moved here and there in the meadow, knee deep in young grass, gathering roses and lilies, crocuses and violets, hyacinths and narcissuses. She made a lovely picture, for she was as pretty as a flower herself. Too pretty, as it turned out, for (so the old Greek poem tells) Pluto, the grim King of the Underworld, pushing his head up out of the earth, fell in love with the young maiden, and, caring nothing for her shrieks and struggles, carried her off to be his queen in the gloomy caverns that were his palace.

Before long the girl's mother, the goddess Demeter, came to look for her, and was exceedingly distressed when she found that she had disappeared. With her golden hair covered by a dark mantle such as widows wore, the goddess searched high and low, here, there, and everywhere. Still she was unsuccessful, until one day the Sun took pity on her tears and anguish, and told her what had happened to Persephone, and where the girl was. Demeter was then very angry indeed. After all, she was a goddess, equal in rank with old Pluto; how dared he steal from her what she treasured most? She resolved to make it quite clear that she was not to be treated in so abominable a fashion, and so (since she was the goddess of corn and of agriculture) she vowed that never would she let the corn sprout in the ground until her daughter had been restored to her safe and sound.

In vain did the oxen drag the heavy ploughs across the fields; in vain did the sower drop the barley seed into the furrows. Nothing came up out of the parched brown earth.

Eventually those in authority began to get worried. The stock of corn in the barns and warehouses was being used up fast, and when it had all gone, what were the people to make into bread? There was every likelihood that before long men would be dying of hunger, and furthermore the gods would be robbed of the sacrifices that they had come to expect as their due. So at last Zeus, the King of the Gods, realized that something must be done before it was too late. He implored Demeter to withdraw her ban, but every appeal was made in vain. Demeter insisted that her daughter must be returned to her. Pluto, too, was not at all helpful; he had captured Persephone and he intended to keep her. At length a compromise was fixed up. Persephone, it was arranged, should spend half the year in the Underworld with Pluto, and the other half with her mother and the gods in the upper world. Every year she should return when the earth was gay with the first flowers of spring, and stay there until the autumn leaves began to fall.

Filled with joy, Persephone returned into the sunshine; and so thrilled was Demeter at the restoration of her daughter that she bade the seed in the ground to sprout and produce a bountiful harvest.

For long afterwards a festival was held every year

33

in the great temple of Demeter at Eleusis, near Athens. It was a " mystery "; that is, only the initiated were allowed to take part in it, and the secret of what occurred was very well kept. But it is supposed that there was a kind of stage play representing the burial of the seed in the ground, followed by the growth of the young corn. Possibly some of the scenes had to do with the life of man beyond the grave; for, it might be argued, just as the seed put in the cold earth grew at last into the ear of wheat, so for men the grave might not be the end: they, too, might be re-born if they had deserved it—not on earth, but in some lovely Paradise, perhaps beyond the sky.

Whatever shape they took, there is little doubt that the " Eleusinian mysteries " were intended as an encouragement and a help to " Mother Nature " —so that she should not make a mistake and fail to send the fruits of each season at the proper time. Perhaps, too, there was just a suggestion of a fear that she—or the gods responsible for managing the earth's affairs—would forget to see that spring came after winter, and summer after spring.

To us such a fear may seem childish and silly enough, but to our ancestors of long ago it was not so. To the primitive savage, writes Sir J. G. Frazer in *The Golden Bough*, with his short memory and imperfect means of measuring the flight of time, a year may well have seemed so long that he failed to see that it was one of a cycle or series at all. He must have watched the changing aspects of earth and sky with a perpetual wonder, now delighted, now alarmed.

In autumn when the withered leaves were whirled about the forest by the nipping blast, and he looked up at the bare boughs, could he feel sure that they would ever be green again ? As day by day the sun sank lower and lower in the sky, could he be certain that the luminary would ever retrace his heavenly road ? Even the waning moon, whose pale sickle rose thinner and thinner every night over the rim of the eastern horizon, may have excited in his mind a fear lest, when it had wholly vanished, there should be moons no more.

With his mind filled with such misgivings it is only natural that man should have done all that lay in his power to " bring back the faded blossom to the bough, to swing the low sun of winter up to his old place in the summer sky, and to restore its orbed fullness to the silver lamp of the waning moon." So he turned to magic, and many of the quaint customs and picturesque ceremonies that were, or still are, practised by the peoples of East and West are survivals of the experiments and attempts by men long ages ago to control the forces of Nature.

Going back to the Persephone story, we can see that the young goddess who spends six months of every year underground and then six months in the light of day may well be a symbol of vegetation, corn in particular, which is buried in the cold earth for some months of every winter and comes to life again in the sprouting cornstalks and the opening leaves and flowers of spring. Demeter, too, is so closely connected with Persephone that the two are both said to personify the corn ; Demeter, as a matter of fact, is styled the Corn Goddess.

Such was the myth in ancient Greece, the story that helped to explain the coming of spring after the long and deathlike sleep of winter. But Greece

35

was not exceptional in this. In many other countries of Europe, even at the present time, we may meet with ceremonies in which a chief part is played by what is called the Corn Mother. "The Corn Mother is running over the field," say the German countryfolk as in springtime the wind ripples through the corn; and when children say that they are going into the field to pull the blue cornflowers and the red poppies, their parents forbid them, since the Corn Mother is sitting in the corn and will snap them up. As we shall see, the Corn Mother has a great part to play in the ceremonies of "harvest home."

Mourning for Adonis

Another of the ancient stories connected with the spring-time is that of Venus and Adonis in Syria. Adonis, we are told, was a very handsome youth who was beloved by the goddess Venus, or Aphrodite as the Greeks called her. As a baby he was so beautiful that the goddess hid him away in a chest, which she entrusted to Persephone, Queen (as we have just seen) of the Underworld. But when Persephone, being curious, peeped into the box and saw the lovely child, she refused to return the box to Aphrodite when she asked for it. The goddess went down into the Underworld to fetch the box and its precious contents, and Persephone at length agreed to just the same arrangement that her mother had made with Pluto: Adonis should live six months of the year with Persephone, and the rest of the year with Aphrodite up above. But alas, one day when he was hunting the wild boar, the brave youth was killed on Mount Lebanon by the fierce beast, and from his blood sprang the scarlet anemone.

Bitterly then did Aphrodite mourn his loss. And not only Aphrodite: all over western Asia and in all the lands where Greek was spoken the death of Adonis was mourned each year. Images of the handsome youth were made, and either buried or thrown into the sea, to the accompaniment of wailing and lamentation and beating of the breast.

But the next day there was an end to grief. Adonis was believed to have come to life again, and to have taken his place in heaven.

Almost the same story was told still earlier by the Babylonians, of a handsome youth named Tammuz, who was beloved by the goddess Ishtar. He, too, was believed to have been carried away into " the land from which no one ever returns, to the house of darkness, where dust lies on door and bolt." He, too, was sought by the goddess, who at length brought him back with her to the upper world. He, too, was mourned each year by the women and girls, and his image, clad in a red robe and washed with pure water and anointed with oil, was thrown into the sea. In the Bible, in the book of Ezekiel, we are given a picture of women " weeping for Tammuz " beside the Temple gate.

Both these old stories, these ancient myths, and others like them, have their origin in the fear that winter will last for ever, that spring will forget to come. The burial is a symbol of the winter sleep ; the coming again, the resurrection, is an expression of the hope (which with us seems a certainty, but did not seem so to those people of long ago) that though winter has come, spring will not be far behind. If winter be slow in ending, then (so the worshippers of Adonis and Tammuz may well have argued) these little ceremonies of ours may serve as a reminder—may, indeed, give old Winter a parting kick and hold out a helping hand to young Spring.

March is usually held to be the first month of Spring; in England, Spring begins—officially—on March 21. In the oldest Roman calendar March was the first month of the year, and in England for centuries the New Year used to begin on March 25; it was not until 1752 that January 1 became New Year's Day in the legal sense, although for general purposes it had been so regarded for a long time. The month is named after the old Roman war-god Mars. But Mars was originally not a god of war but of vegetation, and it was to him that the Roman farmers used to pray for fine harvests of corn and vines and fruit. Even the ceremony held each year in Rome in March, when a band of priests dressed in imposing uniforms and high conical hats went in procession through the city streets, beating their shields with sticks and chanting songs, is supposed to have been intended to drive out the demons and make the corn grow.

The Meaning of Easter

In Christian lands the greatest festival of the whole year is Easter. This, too, is a springtime festival—one commemorating a resurrection after the sleep of death. When Jesus Christ was " cruci-fied, dead, and buried," as the Creed says; when

" on the third day he rose again from the dead," is a matter that has never been definitely decided. From very ancient times, however, this most solemn and yet most happy festival has been celebrated in the earlier part of the year, at about the same time as the death and resurrection of some of the pagan gods was celebrated in the countries that lie around the eastern end of the Mediterranean Sea. Some scholars, indeed, have put forward the theory that the Christian Church in its early days deliberately chose to keep Easter at a time and in a season when the heathen whom it was hoped to convert were already accustomed to worship a god who had died and then risen again to eternal life. Whether this be so or not, there is one thing about Easter that is undeniably non-Christian, and that is its name. The word probably comes from Eostre, who, we are told, was the goddess of the spring or the dawn among the Anglo-Saxons, and whose festival was celebrated in the springtime. This, of course, was before Christianity was brought to England by St. Augustine in A.D. 597—brought for the second time, since during the four hundred years when England was part of the Roman Empire there were many Christians in the land. There is an old legend that the first Christian missionary to arrive in England was Joseph of Arimathaea—he in whose tomb the body of the dead Christ was laid, and who is said to have founded a church at Glastonbury in Somerset. More likely, perhaps, Christianity was introduced by Roman soldiers, who had embraced it while serving in Gaul, as France was then called, or in Italy.

Easter is a " movable feast," that is, it is not

celebrated at the same time every year. Its fixing is a most complicated matter, but to put it shortly, Easter Day is always the first Sunday after the full moon which happens upon, or next after, March 21. (The " full moon " in question is not the real moon, however, but a " calendar moon " invented for the purpose.) The earliest possible day on which Easter can fall is March 22, and the latest April 25. Often there is a wide difference between one year and the next; thus in 1948 Easter Day was on March 28, and in 1949 on April 17, three weeks later. Many times it has been proposed that Easter should be fixed, for instance, on the second Sunday in April; but however irritating the dodging about from March to April may be to holiday-makers, it has so far been impossible to agree on a date that would suit everybody.

The matter is made all the more difficult since there are many other Church festivals whose dates depend on that of Easter. Thus the season of Lent is the period between Ash Wednesday—so called because in the services on that day in some churches ashes are sprinkled on the congregation to remind them that Adam, the first man, is said to have been made out of the dust of the ground, and into dust or ashes men's bodies will return when they die—and Easter Eve ; in this period there are forty weekdays, on which good Christians are expected to fast or practise some other form of self-denial.

The day before Ash Wednesday is Shrove Tuesday, which gets its name from the ancient practice, in the Catholic Church, of confessing one's sins to the priest and receiving from him absolution or forgiveness—what was called in olden days, being shriven. Since it was the day before the beginning of Lent, it was made the occasion of much feasting and jollity. Boys and girls used to call at the houses of all their friends and neighbours, and sang:

Shrovetide is nigh at hand,
And I be come a-shroving;
Pray, dame, something,
An apple or a dumpling.

TOSSING THE PANCAKE AT WESTMINSTER SCHOOL
(*from an old print*)

Another name for Shrove Tuesday is Pancake Day, because on that day the cooks used up the fine flour and fat that they had in the kitchen, in making these delicacies; in Lenten fare there was nothing so fanciful. Still every year a tossing or throwing the pancake is practised in Westminster School. At eleven o'clock the school cook enters the hall, carrying a pancake in a pan. This he cleverly twirls and then throws into the air over a beam in the roof. All the boys scramble for the pancake, and happy indeed is he who manages to secure it unbroken or grabs the largest fragment, for he is awarded a guinea.

The Days of Holy Week

The week before Easter Day, or Easter Sunday, is called Holy Week or Passion Week, because it commemorates the Passion (meaning " suffering ") of Jesus Christ. It begins with Palm Sunday, which commemorates the triumphal entry of Jesus into Jerusalem ; the people, we are told in the Gospel, " took branches of palm trees and went forth to meet Him, crying Hosanna." In Catholic churches branches of palm, or of some other tree such as box, yew, or willow, are blessed by the priest and distributed among the congregation after Mass ; sometimes they are carried in procession through the streets. Then they are collected and burnt, and the ashes are kept to be sprinkled on the heads of the people on Ash Wednesday of the following year.

The Thursday in Holy Week is called Holy Thursday, or Maundy Thursday. " Maundy " is said to come from an old word meaning " basket " ; the poor used to bring baskets with them to take away the good things. Formerly on Maundy Thursday it was the custom in England for the King to wash the feet of a number of poor men, in imitation of the action of Christ in washing His disciples' feet on the eve of His Passion. The last English sovereign to carry out the ceremony in person was James II. Subsequently presents of food and drink and clothing were made instead.

For a great many years gifts of money have been made, and special Maundy money is coined by the Mint. In Rome there is still a ceremonial washing of the feet of a number of priests by the Pope.

Next follows Good Friday, the most solemn day in the Christian year, since it was on this day that Christ was crucified and His dead body was laid in the tomb. In most Christian churches services of a deeply moving character are held; for three hours the incidents of the Passion are commemorated in turn, and (in Catholic worship) the lights are put out one by one, until only one is left, hidden away beside the altar. Comes Holy Saturday; and then dawns Easter Day, or Easter Sunday, the day of triumph.

MAUNDY MONEY

What a contrast with Good Friday! If, for instance, we were to go into the greatest church in Christendom—St. Peter's, Rome—on Good Friday, we should note that there were signs of deep mourning all around. Neither the Pope nor his cardinals would be wearing their rings of office; their dress would be purple, the colour of grief. The Papal Guard would carry their arms reversed as at a funeral. We might see the Pope, shoeless, kneeling in prayer before a partially veiled crucifix. The music would be of the most solemn kind. But on Easter Sunday everything is just the opposite. Early in the morning cannon fired from the ramparts

43

would announce the glad tidings. St. Peter's we should find a blaze of light. The cardinals would be glittering figures in their magnificent robes, and the Pope would be carried in his high chair to celebrate Mass, and then from the balcony give his blessing to the thousands assembled below. The music would suggest joyous victory.

Not the least impressive of the Easter ceremonies is the midnight service in an Eastern Orthodox church, in Russia perhaps, or in Greece. For an hour before twelve on the Saturday night there is solemn chanting by the choir. Then all the lights are lowered, and the music dies away into little more than a whisper. But as twelve strikes, the lights go up again, the organ and the choir burst into a hymn of triumph, and the priests and members of the congregation kiss 'each other and say " Christ is risen," to which the reply is " Christ is risen indeed !"

In olden days there was many a strange custom at Easter-tide—customs which owed nothing to Christianity, but were survivals of the days of paganism. Most of these have fallen into disuse, but we still have on Good Friday our hot-cross buns and on Easter Sunday our Easter eggs. None can say for certain what was the origin of the one or the other. One suggestion is that the eating of cross-buns may be traced to a pagan custom of worshipping the chief goddess, the " Queen of Heaven," with little cakes—a custom which may be found in China and ancient Mexico and other lands. As for the eggs, it is said that, again from very ancient times, eggs, brightly coloured, have been regarded as emblems of resurrection.

Eating the Passover

The crucifixion of Christ coincided, we are told, with a great Jewish feast or festival, that of the Passover, that commemorates the escape of the Children of Israel from bondage in the land of Egypt; just before their departure the destroying angel of Jehovah (the God of the Hebrews) visited the houses of the Egyptians and slew all the first-born, but the houses of the Israelites or Hebrews he passed over.

Passover is celebrated annually in the first month of the Jewish ecclesiastical or religious year—Nisan, as it is called, corresponding to parts of March and April. Unlike Easter, Passover (or Pasch as the Jews call it) is a fixed feast, and is the occasion for a great family gathering and reunion, very much as Christmas is with the Gentiles (the Jews' name for non-Jews).

The festival lasts eight days. On the night before the first evening, that is, on 14th Nisan, the house is gone through to make sure that no leaven or bread is to be found; if any is found, it has to be burnt the next morning. There follows a special service in the synagogue or church, after which the family sit down to the Passover meal—the Seder, it is called. (The Last Supper of Jesus and His disciples in the upper room at Jerusalem was the Seder.) The table in the dining-room will be covered with a cloth, the lamps lit, and plates laid round. In the centre will be dishes containing bitter herbs, symbolizing the misery that the Israelites had to endure when they were slaves in Egypt; Passover cakes made of unleavened bread in accordance with the instruction given to the Israelites on the first Passover ; and the shank bone of a lamb—this being just a remembrance of the Passover lamb which in former times was specially sacrificed. The master of the house opens the ceremony with a prayer of blessing, and then the company eat from the dishes and drink cups of wine, and at the proper times sing hymns and psalms. The youngest child asks his father in Hebrew, " What is the meaning of this ceremony ? ", and the father replies, " We were slaves in Egypt, and the Lord our God has brought us out with a mighty hand and a stretched-out arm." All then repeat the story of the departure from Egypt, as it is given in the book of Exodus in the Bible. During the rest of the week there are more ceremonial meals and services in the synagogues, and the women take advantage of the opportunity to arrange marriages for the young people.

Festival of the Dolls

Such, then, are some of the religious festivals and ceremonies that mark the springtime of the year, but many a volume would be needed to describe the ways in which the peoples of so many different countries rejoice over the delightful change in the seasons. Some of them will be mentioned when we arrive at the month of May, but here we may take a peep at one of the strangest of the springtime customs. The place is the Indian state of Udaipur, in Rajputana. Here in early spring takes place the Festival of the Dolls. The women of the city, who for the rest of the year are kept in strict purdah (that is, practically shut up in their homes and heavily veiled), are given a day of comparative freedom. Each woman carries a doll—whether it be an expensive, elaborately-dressed creation or a few rags wrapped round a stick—and they crowd the streets and line the river bank from early morning until it begins to get dark. The greatest event of the day is when the prince, having ridden through the streets on an elephant, embarks in his state barge and is rowed round the lake in full view of his loyal subjects. With eager eyes the women watch the procession, and then the prince returns to the seclusion of his palace and the women go back with dragging feet to the homes that must sometimes seem like prisons.

APRIL

DO you see them coming down that grassy slope, some riding but most of them on foot, past the chapel on the hill to the ford that leads across the river? There is the " very perfit gentil knight," and riding beside him his son, " a yong Squyer, a lover, and a lusty bacheler, with lokkes curled as if they lay in presse "; there are the yeoman in his gay green coat with a sheaf of arrows across his back, and the monk whose delight is in hunting the hare, and the merry friar, who can sing and play the flute; there is the " Clerk of Oxenford," who is so proud of his " twenty bookes, clothed in blak and red, of Aristotil, and his philosophie " that stand beside his bed at home; and there is the coy Prioress, whose table manners are so perfect and whose heart is so kind that " she wolde weepe if that she saw a mous caught in a trappe. . . ." Yes, and there go the Carpenter, the Miller and the Reeve, the Doctor of Physic, the Merchant, the Dyer, the Cook and the Shipman, and—yes, there is the " Wif of Bathe," with her red stockings and new shoes, her red face and bold looks, " a worthy womman al her lyfe, Husbondes at chirche dore hadde she fyfe." Slowly they go by, chattering and clattering, cracking jokes, and now and again breaking out into song. Down the hill they go, and splashing through the water. And as they emerge on the further bank and shake the water out of their shoes and straighten their dress, the mist comes up and hides them, and they are gone. For it is getting on for six hundred years now since Chaucer told how

> When that Aprille with his showres swoot
> The drought of March hath perced to the root,
> . . . . from every shires ende
> Of Engelond, to Canturbury they wende . . .

For many centuries the " Canterbury Pilgrims " made their way to the magnificent tomb of Archbishop Thomas Becket, slain in his cathedral in 1170 by four of King Henry's knights, who took too literally their master's hastily-spoken wish that someone would rid him of an " unruly priest." Becket as a man had many enemies, but as a martyr and a saint he attracted the love of the multitude. All the same, it was not only religious devotion that impelled the crowds along all the roads that led to Canterbury. There was also the spirit of adventure —for it *was* an adventure to leave one's town or village in those days ; there was the desire to " see the world " in good company, to break the monotony of a daily life in which there were few amusements and none of the comforts that we have come to look upon as necessaries. The Canterbury Pilgrims are only the most famous of an immense crowd of men and women and children who for many hundreds of years, in most countries of the world, have left their homes for a few days or weeks or months at a time, and gone on pilgrimage to some holy city, the grave of some particularly saintly saint, or some church or other place where (so it was believed) miracles of healing might be expected. In Europe, in those Dark Ages that followed upon the collapse of the

" A WORTHY WOMMAN AL HER LYFE "

" A VERY PERFIT GENTIL KNIGHT "

" A LUSTY BACHELER, WITH LOKKES CURLED "

" IF THAT SHE SAW A MOUS "

50

Roman Empire, there were few travellers who were not pilgrims, and vast numbers of people of all classes walked the hundreds of miles to Rome to see the Pope, or the yet greater distance to the Holy Land of Palestine, to visit the actual places where Jesus had lived and taught—Bethlehem, where He was said to have been born ; Nazareth, where He lived as a boy and helped His father in the carpenter's shop ; the Sea of Galilee, on which He sailed in the fishing-boats, and Jerusalem, which was the scene of the Passion. Many difficulties and dangers had to be faced, particularly by the pilgrims to Palestine after that land was overrun by the Turks, who were not Christians, but Mohammedans. However, they thought the journey well worth while, since their sins were thereby supposed to be forgiven and they had the chance of buying at Jerusalem a tiny piece of the cross on which Jesus had been crucified—at least the man who sold the splinter *said* there was no doubt of its being genuine—or a finger-bone of some saint which was supposed to be a remarkable wonder-worker. Besides, the man who had been to the Holy Land and returned home safely was very highly thought of by his friends and neighbours ; he was called a palmer, because of the palm leaf that he carried as a sign to convince the doubters that he really had been to foreign parts.

Another place that drew a great crowd of pilgrims was the shrine or tomb of St. James, one of the disciples of Jesus and the patron saint of Spain, at Santiago de Compostella, in the north-western corner of the peninsula. All pilgrims who had visited it were entitled to wear a scallop-shell in their hat or pinned on their cloak; and to this custom may be traced, strangely enough, the making of " grottoes " by London children on St. James's Day (July 25). " Mind the grotto! " calls out the guardian of the little heap of oyster-shells, and he hopes to receive a penny—but he probably knows nothing about St. James.

Nor is the custom dead by any means. It is very likely that more people go on pilgrimage in Europe today than in the Middle Ages. Some of them still go on foot, but the great majority take advantage of the special excursion-tickets issued by the railways.

At Bernadette's Grotto in Lourdes

Probably the most popular of all the places visited by present-day Christian pilgrims is Lourdes, a small town in the south-western corner of France. Here in 1858 a young girl named Bernadette Soubirous, the daughter of working-class parents living in the poorest part of the town, was gathering firewood near a grotto or cave when she had a vision of a very beautiful Lady with golden hair and dressed in white, with a blue girdle about her waist. Several times Bernadette saw the Lady sitting in the grotto, and at first everyone to whom she told her story laughed and said she was romancing. Then one day the Lady told her to wash herself in the spring and drink of the water. Bernadette looked around, and at first could not see any spring, but soon water came bubbling up out of the rock and formed a pool. People now began to believe that her story was not so silly as they had thought, and when (so it was claimed) a child, supposed to be at death's door, was dipped in the pool and taken out cured, there was a great rush of sick folk to the grotto. Now it came to be generally agreed that a lady really had appeared to little Bernadette, and that she was none other than the Virgin Mary, the mother of Jesus Christ. A church was built above the grotto, and then another down below, and from all parts of the world thousands and thousands of

BERNADETTE'S GROTTO AT LOURDES

Catholic Christians—those Christians, that is, who belong to the Roman Catholic Church—began to flock to the miraculous shrine at Lourdes. (Bernadette herself became a nun, and after a long and painful illness died in 1879; in 1933 she was declared to be a saint in heaven.)

Still the pilgrimages to Lourdes go on. In Catholic churches you may see posters giving particulars of cheap trips for pilgrims; special trains are run from all parts, carrying pilgrims who are well but still more pilgrims who suffer from some complaint—cripples and consumptives, epileptics, the paralysed and the blind. Having arrived in Lourdes, the pilgrims walk in long processions to the grotto and its two churches, and those who cannot walk are pushed in their invalid-chairs or carried on stretchers. It is dreadfully sad to see them go by, dusty and tired and so ill, and yet on their faces there is a look of hope, of expected joy. On reaching the grotto, they lie closely packed on the stairs and terrace, drinking the ice-cold water from little cups, singing hymns, and listening to the prayers. Inside the grotto one may see hanging up numbers of crutches that have been left behind by pilgrims who needed them when they came to Lourdes but needed them no longer when they went away. For people *are* cured at Lourdes, particularly people suffering from what are called nervous complaints.

Such a case was Marie, the young French girl who is the heroine of the novel called *Lourdes* written by the famous French novelist, Emile Zola. She was three-and-twenty, and since she fell from a horse at the age of fourteen she had spent most of her time lying on her back, filled with aches and pains, in a kind of narrow box. The doctors said she was suffering from paralysis. (But one doctor maintained that it was really a case of shock. Zola himself thought that the cures at Lourdes were not miracles, but were due to " faith-healing " or " autosuggestion.") At last she persuaded her father and Pierre, her friend, to take her to Lourdes, and there we see her, lying in her box, and watching with eager eyes the priests carrying the Blessed Sacrament (what Catholics believe to be the Body and Blood of Jesus Christ) in a golden case that shines like the sun. As the procession goes by, a paralytic woman rises and throws aside her crutches. A piercing yell, and another woman, wrapped in a white blanket, stands up on her mattress, and the people say that she is a consumptive who only a moment ago seemed half-dead. Then a blind woman says she can see the grotto, and a dumb woman sinks on her knees and says aloud a prayer of thankfulness to the Virgin, to Our Lady of Lourdes, who has that very moment given her back her speech.

But Pierre had not taken his eyes off Marie. Her poor pale face was contracted as if she were suffering frightfully. She did not speak in her despair. . . . But all at once, when the Blessed Sacrament passed by, a sensation of dizziness came over her. She imagined herself struck by lightning. . . . Her face became animated, suffused with colour, beaming with a smile of joy and health. And, suddenly, Pierre saw her rise, stand upright in her little car, staggering, stuttering. . . . He hurriedly drew near to support her. But she drove him backward with a gesture. She was regaining strength, looking so touching, so beautiful, in the little black woollen gown and slippers which she always wore ; tall and slender, too, and crowned as with a halo of gold by her beautiful flaxen hair, which was covered with a simple piece of lace. . . . " I am cured !—I am cured ! "

With the Pilgrims to Mecca

Of all the places to which people go on pilgrimage the most famous is Mecca, a city in Arabia some forty miles inland from the Red Sea. Indeed, if you look it up in the dictionary, you will find " Mecca " described as " Mohammed's birthplace," and also as " a place which one regards as supremely sacred, or which it is the aspiration of one's life to be able to visit." Certainly, all the many millions of Mohammedans, or Moslems as they are also called, have a great desire to visit the city where the Prophet Mohammed was born in A.D. 570 ; indeed, to make the pilgrimage to Mecca is one of the chief duties imposed on Moslems by their religion. Every Moslem worthy of the name, who can possibly manage it, must make the journey at least once in his lifetime ; when he has done so, he has the honourable title of Hajji, and may wear a green turban. Every year from every corner of the Moslem world crowds of pilgrims set out for Mecca, travelling by railway or by steamship, in camel caravans or on foot. Nowadays some may go by air. Arabs, Indians, and Malays, Negroes from all parts of Africa, Persians and Turks, Egyptians, Syrians, Chinese—they pour into the holy city. Occasionally a white face is seen among them, for some Englishmen have been converted to Islam. But the great majority of the pilgrims are brown or yellow or black.

If we could join them, we should arrive at Jeddah, the port on the Red Sea, and then make the last part of the journey to Mecca on donkeys or camels, or, if we are very poor, on foot. Before we got near the city we should have to take off our ordinary clothes and put on the *ihram*, or pilgrim's robe, consisting of two small blankets, one of which is wrapped round the waist and the other flung over the shoulders. In spite of the fierce sun, no hat or turban may be worn, and only heel-less slippers may be put on the feet. When dressed in this way, a man is a pilgrim, and bound by the pilgrims' rules; thus he may not hunt or catch birds—though he may fish, and he is not permitted to kill even a flea. (But if a fierce dog attacks him, he may try to kill it in self-defence.) Then he must be very careful not to use bad language, or to pick quarrels, or to speak to a woman unless it is absolutely necessary.

THE HOLY CARPET ARRIVING AT MECCA

When they have entered the holy city the pilgrims should keep to a carefully arranged programme. First they go to the great mosque (or church), where in the middle of the courtyard stands the Kaaba, considered by Moslems to be the holiest building in the world. It is like a big cube, and is covered with a rich carpet—a new one is sent by the King of Egypt every year—and in one corner is the Black Stone, which Moslems believe fell from heaven when Adam was created, and was put where it is now by Abraham, when he built the Kaaba ages ago. (Very likely it is a meteorite, and so did

E 57

really " fall from heaven " !). The pilgrims must go round the Kaaba seven times, three times running or walking very fast, and then four times at an ordinary pace; they begin at the Black Stone corner, and every time they kiss the stone with great devotion, or touch it with a hand and then kiss that. Originally, so it is said, it was whiter than milk, but it has been kissed by so many millions of sinful men that it is now quite black; it is supposed, however, to be still as white as ever inside. Anyone who finds Arabic a difficult language to learn, may go down a few steps and kiss the foundation-stone of the Kaaba, when (so it is said) he will find the task of learning very much easier.

Next, the well Zem-Zem must be visited. This is close to the Kaaba, and it is supposed to be the very same well of water that, as we are told in the first book of the Bible, bubbled up in the desert just in time to save Hagar and her son Ishmael—from whom the Arabs claim to be descended—from a horrible death. Just as Hagar ran or staggered with her child to the spring that had miraculously appeared in the sands, so the pilgrims must run along what is believed to be the same path; and as they go panting and blowing they try to say the prayers that are required of them. The water of " Hagar's Well " is not very tasty, but good Moslems drink as much as they possibly can of it. Some even bathe in it as well.

Among the other places that must be visited is the room in which the Prophet was born, and the custom is to pour a little scent on the stone which marks where his cradle stood. Then several days are passed in visits to sacred places in the neighbourhood and in listening to sermons.

One of the strangest performances is that in the valley of Mina; here there are three marks or pillars, and every pilgrim must throw seven stones at them as he goes by. Why, is not altogether clear; some Moslems say that it is because it is here that Abraham threw stones at the Devil, who was trying to interrupt his prayers, and some say it was Adam who first started the custom. When the stones have been thrown, the pilgrims may slay a goat or a sheep, a cow or a camel, and make a feast, to which their friends are invited; any of the good fare that is left over is given to the poor. Next there should be a visit to the barber for a head-shave, and with this the pilgrimage is officially ended.

But most of the pilgrims make another visit to the Kaaba; and those who have the time to spare, and sufficient money left in their purse, go on to the city of Medina, about 250 miles to the north of Mecca, where Mohammed died in A.D. 632; there they will certainly visit the Mosque of the Prophet, which contains the tomb in which his body is believed to be lying, the face turned towards Mecca.

In India's Holiest City

Mecca is the holy city of the Moslems, and Jerusalem of the Jews. The holiest city in India is Benares, on the Ganges, the holiest of rivers. For more than two thousand years vast crowds have flocked to worship in its hundreds of temples and shrines, and (if they are so lucky) to die within the circuit of a certain road. For (so it is believed) he who dies in holy Benares goes straight to one of the heavens that Hindus believe in, or at least he may be sure of being reincarnated in a happier shape, a nicer body, than the one he has just finished with. All along the banks of the great river (which is thought of as a goddess, and is said to flow from the toe of Vishnu, one of the three great Hindu gods, or from the brow of Siva, another one of the " triad ") are terraces, or ghats, as they are called. On the Burning Ghat the bodies of the dead are burnt so that the ashes may be thrown into the river. Many of the pilgrims bring with them the ashes of relatives who have died and been cremated in their home town. Sometimes ashes are sent to the authorities by parcel-post, with a request that they should be flung into the sacred stream.

What a sight it is, on any and every day of the year, but more especially at the height of the pilgrimage season ! Some who have seen it, have bluntly called it horrible ; some have said they were fascinated, finding it strangely beautiful. For three miles the city stretches along the river—three miles of towering temples and magnificent palaces and the most squalid slums. It is crammed full of people. Some are sitting in deep thought, staring at the tips of their noses ; but the great mass are wandering about, buying and selling, making merry or mourning the dead, boating and bathing in the river, which, if truth be told, is exceedingly dirty. (But all the same, many a worshipper makes a cup of his hands and takes a mouthful.)

Some years ago Mr. Aldous Huxley was in Benares at the time of an eclipse of the sun ; a million and more Hindus had flocked into the city to see a serpent in the sky try to swallow the sun, and to do all in their power to help the " Light of Heaven " against his enemy. Mr. Huxley was much more interested in watching the people than in what was happening in the sky. From his boat he looked up at acres on acres of them, crowded on the ghats above the river. He saw come staggering down through the crowd a palanquin carried on the shoulders of six attendants in bright red liveries. It was set down, and out of it scurried several ladies into a great barge, like a Noah's Ark, with scarlet window-curtains, that floated at the water's edge. When the barge had been pushed out into the river, the ladies inside were bold enough to pull aside the curtains and look out with unabashed curiosity at the passing boats and " our inquisitive camera." Poor princesses (remarks Mr. Huxley), they were not allowed to bathe with their lowly-born but un-imprisoned sisters in the open Ganges. *Their* dip was to be in the barge's bilge water. . . .

Then there were the beggars. In India it is a religious duty and one of the best of good deeds to give alms, and on every hand the beggars abound, many of them not just poor and dirty and old, but horribly repulsive with exposed sores and mutila-tions. The narrow lanes that lead from the ghats to the open streets in the centre of the town were lined with beggars more or less holy, says Mr. Huxley. They sat on the ground with their begging-bowls before them ; the charitable, as they passed, would throw a few grains of rice into each of the bowls, and by the end of the day the beggars might, with luck, have collected enough for a square meal. Then from an archway emerged a sacred bull, lowered his muzzle to the bowl of a sleeping beggar, made a scouring movement with his black tongue, and—a morning's charity had gone! The beggar still dozed, as, thoughtfully chewing, the bull turned away and disappeared.*

To Benares in the Morning

Not everyone who sets out as a pilgrim to the holy city reaches Benares. Many die on the way of old age or sickness, and their ashes are collected by their friends and tipped into the Ganges on their arrival. Some are too young. In the highest of the great castes or divisions of the Hindu people—the Brahman—every boy on reaching a certain age is expected to pretend to set out for Benares. He takes in his hand a ball of sweets tied in a cloth, slings a little bundle holding his few clothes and belongings on a bamboo pole across his shoulder, and boldly sets out, accompanied by his relatives and friends, who make music on various instruments. He has not gone far when he is held up by seven streaks of water that his *guru* or teacher has made across the road; these are supposed to represent the seven oceans, and the boy has to worship them, offering flowers and nuts and a few of the smallest coins. The teacher also warns him of the many hardships that lie ahead, and asks him if he would not prefer to turn back? But the boy is not to be frightened, and says that his mind is fully

* See Aldous Huxley, *Jesting Pilate* (Chatto & Windus).

made up and he is determined to get to Benares. "Then," says the teacher, "you had better hurry," and he pushes him along the path he must follow. But he has gone only a few steps when his uncle or father or friend, who has gone on ahead, steps out from the path, catches the boy up, and takes him in his arms or puts him on his horse, and sees him safely home again. Years later, perhaps, the boy, having become a man, will set out again, and then no grown-up will be there to pounce out and put a sudden end to his adventures.

Spring in Cherry-blossom Land

It is still springtime, and what better season of the year to visit Japan, the land of cherry-blossom, when the sun shines bright and the lovely snow-capped cone of Mount Fuji is seen against the light blue sky? At all times of the year the roads and footpaths in Japan seem filled with pilgrims, but it is when winter has said "good-bye" that the young people in particular love to leave their homes in the crowded cities and make for the temples and shrines of the countryside.

They are a jolly band, far different from the deeply-serious Moslems whom we have glimpsed kissing the Black Stone in the Kaaba, and the Hindus bathing in the dark waters of the Ganges. The boys are in shorts and open-neck shirts, the girls in brightly coloured kimonos or perhaps—for they are keen on Western fashions—in skirt and blouse. They sing as they go along, they joke and play, and it is quite plain that they are "pilgrimaging" for the fun of the thing rather than for any deep religious reason. Most young people belong to a pilgrim society, and they save up all the year long for their annual jaunt.

When the great day of their holiday comes, they meet in a temple courtyard, choose a leader, and then set out, each with a tiny straw hat and sandals hanging by a string round the neck, and some holding a long bamboo stick. When they get to a shrine or holy place they march through the *torii*— a decorated gateway, made of a tree-trunk placed across two upright posts, which is believed to keep the devils away—into the courtyard before the little temple. There is a bell, which they ring to attract the gods' attention, or they clap their hands to wake them up; then they bow their heads, say a short prayer, or just think seriously on religious matters for a few minutes. This done, they pour out into the road again, and go laughing on their way. But before they go, they make sure of getting a ticket from the priest in charge of the shrine, which they will keep as evidence that they have really been there.

A Visit to the Sun-Goddess

There are thousands and thousands of different gods and goddesses and spirits of one kind or another in Japan, and each has his or her shrine or temple or holy place. But the most important is the shrine at Ise of the Sun-Goddess. Her name is Amaterasu-Omikami, and Japanese schoolboys and schoolgirls are told by their teachers that she is not only the chief of the *Kami* (gods) but is the ever-so-many greats-grandmother of the Emperor. They are also told, and may read in the Japanese history-books, that she was the daughter of the first two gods that ever were, Izanagi and Izanami, who made Japan, its islands, mountains, trees and grass, and the sea round about. From the beginning it was intended that Amaterasu should be the ruler of Japan. She divided the land from the water, taught the people how to grow and cook rice, and gave them their first lessons in making silk. She was as bright and good as the sun in the sky, and she was indeed the Sun-Goddess. After a time she made her grandson Jimmu the first emperor, and from him the present Imperial Family of Japan claim to be descended in an unbroken line.

At Ise is her " Grand Imperial Shrine." It is nothing much to look at—just a group of thatched wooden huts enclosed by a high fence—but it is very old, and very, very holy ; inside is the sacred mirror which the Sun-Goddess is said to have given to her grandson, telling him to " look upon this mirror as me, myself, and always revere it." At certain times of the year—in the spring when the seed is about to be put into the ground, in the summer when the first fruits are being gathered, and at the harvest festival in the autumn—the Emperor sends special messengers with gifts to the Ise shrine, and whenever there is some great happening it is reported to the Sun-Goddess there. One of the first things a new emperor does is to pay his respects to her by a personal visit to Ise.

Once in a lifetime every Japanese is supposed to visit Ise, just as Moslems are expected to visit Mecca. Pilgrims to any and every shrine in Japan may take away with them " god tickets " or lucky charms, but the charms sold by the priests at Ise are supposed to be particularly powerful for good. They consist of tiny boxes, less than an inch long and not a quarter of an inch thick, wrapped in white paper and sealed with the official seal; inside is the charm, which is nothing more than a piece of wood wrapped in white paper. But it is not ordinary wood. What is supposed to make it so precious is that it comes from the temple itself, since this is rebuilt every twenty years. Thus the man who buys one of these charms can carry about with him a piece of the very house in which the Sun-Goddess has lived. Surely, he thinks, that must bring him the very best of good fortune!

The First April Fool

We began this chapter with the Canterbury Pilgrims setting out in April, and the " wander-lust " has carried us far. No one can say for certain where the name " April " comes from. One suggestion is that it derives from the Latin *omnia aperit*, " it opens everything," which seems likely enough when we see the buds on the boughs and the fresh flowers in the meadows and hedgerows. Another suggestion is that there is some connection with the Greek goddess Aphrodite, since the month was sacred to her. Yet another guess—it is no more— is that in ancient times there was a god named Aper or Aprus. The origin of the name is a mystery —and so, too, is the origin of April Fool's Day.

As everyone knows, April 1 is the day when you try to play some harmless trick on someone who is not so sure of the date as you are. In days gone by there have been cases of servant-girls sending some young fellow to a bookshop to buy a copy of the " History of Eve's Grandmother," or to a chemist's for a " bottle of pigeon's milk " ; and little boys have been " caught out " when their elder brothers have told them to go and watch some statue come down from its pedestal when the clock strikes a certain hour. " April fool! " is a jeering cry that we all have heard. In France *poisson d'Avril*, "April fish," means the same thing, and in Scotland the victim is called a " gowk." But what is the reason for it? " Oh, don't you know? " replies some bright spirit; " it's because Noah in the Ark sent out the dove to find the dry ground that wasn't there ! " So Noah's dove was the first April Fool !

MAY

" YOU must wake and call me early, call me early,
mother dear," bids little Alice in one of
Tennyson's poems that almost everybody knows.

I sleep so sound all night, mother, that I shall never wake,
If you do not call me loud when the day begins to break:
But I must gather knots of flowers, and buds and garlands gay,
For I'm to be Queen of the May, mother, I'm to be Queen of the
    May.

How many a little girl has lain in bed on the last
night in April, too excited to sleep, her mind filled
with the thought of May-day morning, when she
will be dressed in her prettiest frock, and escorted
to her throne set in some garden or grassy glade!
There she will be crowned with flowers, and round
the Queen of the May the lads and lassies will hold
hands and dance and sing. Some of them will
perhaps have been up long before, and have gone
a-Maying into the woods to gather flowers and
branches of hawthorn or may—very much as did the
young ladies in *A Midsummer Night's Dream*, who
" rose up early to observe the rites of May," and the
milkmaids whom Samuel Pepys met on his way to
Westminster on May 1, 1667, who " had garlands
upon their pails, and were dancing with a fiddler
before them." Even in London suburbs the May
Queen is still elected every May-day morning, and
crowned and served by courtiers with all the old-
time courtesies. Some people have said that the

May Queen is a reminder of the worship of Flora, the Roman goddess of flowers, whose festival (known as the Floralia) was celebrated on April 28.

Yet if you meet one of your friends who is making plans for getting married, she will very likely tell you that " May is an unlucky month for a wedding." Probably she will not be able to tell you why, and in fact we have to go a long way back in history to find the answer. The month is ill-omened for marriages, says Ovid, the great Roman poet who lived nineteen hundred years ago, because during its course we Romans perform the ceremonies of the Lemuria, held to please the ghosts of the dead and make them favourably disposed towards us. It is Ovid, too, who gives several explanations of the name of the month ; one of them is that it comes from the name of the goddess Maia, who was a wife of Jupiter, the King of the Gods, and mother of the gods Hermes and Mercury.

Dancing round the May-pole

Another May-day custom which seems indeed to be an essential part of " Merrie England " is dancing round the May-pole. In the days of " Good Queen Bess " and of the Stuart Kings, and under the Georges, it flourished exceedingly, and today it has been revived as providing an opportunity for practising the old country dances. But the Puritans of Cromwell's time detested the May-pole, and whenever they had the power they ordered that the poles should be cut down and burnt. They could see nothing good in the custom ; on the contrary, they declared that it was an invention of the Evil One to lead men and girls astray. Here is how one Puritan writer—Philip Stubbes, in a book published in 1583 —describes the May-pole in his day, which was in Queen Elizabeth's reign.

Against May, Whitsunday, or other time, all the young men and maids, old men and wives, run gadding over night to the woods, groves, hills, and mountains, where they spend all the night in pleasant pastimes ; and in the morning they return, bringing with them birch and branches of trees, to deck their assemblies withal. . . . But the chiefest jewel they bring from thence is their May-pole, which they bring home with great veneration, as thus. They have twenty or forty yoke of oxen, every ox having a sweet nosegay of flowers placed on the tip of his horns, and these oxen draw home this May-pole (this stinking idol, rather), which is covered all over with flowers and herbs, bound round about with strings, from the top to the bottom, and sometime painted with variable colours, with two or three hundred men, women, and children following it with great devotion. And thus being reared up, with handkerchiefs and flags hovering on the top, they straw the ground round about, bind green boughs about it, set up summer halls, bowers, and arbours hard by it. And then fall they to dance about it, like as the heathen people did at the dedication of the Idols, whereof this is a perfect pattern, or rather the thing itself.

So writes indignant Mr. Stubbes, and it must be admitted that he made a very good guess at the origin of the May-pole, even though the people whom he criticized so strongly were not really idolaters, nor (we may be sure) were they anything like as bad as he paints them. Beyond a doubt, the May-pole and the rites and ceremonies of which it was the centre were survivals of one of the oldest and most widespread of pagan customs—the worship of trees.

To the savage and to primitive man, the world

around is filled with spirits. There are spirits in the winds and waters and rocks ; animals, like men, have souls, and so have plants and trees. The Redskins who used to roam the vast American plains believed that every kind of tree, shrub, plant, and herb had its own spirit, and at certain times they used to say " thank you " to them for providing them with so many useful materials. In the African jungle and in the islands of the East Indies the natives used to apologize to the tree they were about to cut down for timber or firewood. After a long, long time men reached the idea that the spirit is not the tree, but lives in the tree ; and then, later still, they came to think that the tree-spirit can live in a particular branch, or may even take human shape. But whatever form the tree-spirit takes, it has the power of making the rain to fall and the sun to shine, and makes it easy for lambs and calves to be born—yes, and babies too.

Remembering these beliefs about the tree-spirit, we shall not find it difficult to understand the deeper meaning of the May-tide ceremonies. When the young people go out before dawn on May-day morning to pick branches and adorn themselves with nosegays and crowns of flowers, they are doing what their ancestors of long, long ago used to do at this time of the year ; the difference is that they do not believe, as their ancestors believed, that the tree-spirit has actually his home in the lovely branch of may that they bring back as if in triumph. When in certain places little girls go round on the 1st of May from door to door, wearing garlands, carrying a flower-decked doll, and singing some such song as

this, which used to be sung on May-day morning
by the young folk of Abingdon, in Berkshire—

> We've been a-rambling all the night
>   And sometime of this day;
> And now returning back again,
>   We bring a garland gay.
>
> A garland gay we bring you here;
>   And at your door we stand;
> 'Tis nothing but a sprout, but 'tis well budded out,
>   The work of our Lord's hand—

when they act thus, they are following the ancient
custom of bringing in the tree-spirit. When, as
people still do in France, a May-tree is planted
on May-day morning before each front door, or on
May-eve a big branch is set up against the house
wall, it is again the tree-spirit who is being brought
in from the woods to bless those inside the house,
and make them and all they possess fruitful and
prosperous. And in just the same way was the
May Queen herself thought of originally as being
the tree-spirit's temporary home. These customs
are relics of the tree-worship that our far-distant
forefathers practised in days when all southern
England and most of Europe formed one huge, dense
forest, dark and gloomy, the haunt of fierce beasts
and sometimes of fiercer men.

A Gift 'for the May'

In Catholic countries May is called the month of
the Virgin Mary, and sometimes it is she who is
supposed to be represented by the May Queen.
Here is a story told nearly a hundred years ago of a
beautiful May-day custom in France.

One morning I went out with my mother to call upon a friend. When we had taken a few steps, she said: "Today is the first of May; if the customs of my childhood are still kept up here, we shall see some Mays on our road." "Mays," I said, "what are they?" My mother replied by pointing to the opposite side of the street. "Why, there," she said, "there's a May." Under the arch of the old church porch

A MAY-QUEEN'S BOWER IN A FRENCH VILLAGE
(*from an old print*)

a narrow step was raised, covered with palms. Seated on it was a figure, dressed in a white robe and crowned with flowers; in her right hand was a leafy branch, and over her head was a canopy formed of garlands of box. "Because the month of May is the month of spring," explained my mother, "the month of flowers, the month consecrated to the Virgin, the young girls of each village join together to celebrate its return. They choose a pretty child, and dress her as you see; they seat her on a throne of greenery, crown her, and make her a sort of goddess. She is May, the Virgin of May, the Virgin of lovely days, flowers, and

F   73

green branches. See, there are girls begging of the passers-by." One of them came up to us, and shyly said, "For the May." My mother stopped, and drawing some money from her purse, laid it on the china saucer that the girl held out. As for myself, I took a handful of halfpence, all that I could find in my pocket, and gave them with delight.

Dressing the Wells

From time immemorial May has been considered the appropriate month for visiting the wells whose waters are believed to have the power of curing the sick. The ancient Greeks and Romans had their holy wells, which they regarded with religious reverence ; in fact, wells and streams and rivers were deemed to be the abode of spirits who had it in their power to make the water to flow or to hold it back. Some of the most charming figures of the old mythologies are the nymphs who were supposed to haunt the water side. In Eastern countries there is no more welcome sight than a palmy oasis in the heart of the desert. It is not surprising, then, that men should have devised ceremonies intended to honour the divinities who had the water in their charge. The most famous instance still surviving in England, after no one can say how many centuries, is the well-dressing ceremony at the Derbyshire village of Tissington, near Ashbourne. Here on Ascension Day each year the wells are adorned with flowers, arranged so as to make a beautiful and intricate pattern. Usually a text from the Bible is placed at the top, and below there is a picture of some Biblical scene. There are five wells ; each has a different picture, and a religious service is held at each in turn. It is said that the custom originated in the fourteenth century, when Tissington was the only village in Derbyshire that was not afflicted by an epidemic of the Black Death. But there are a number of other wells in the county and elsewhere which are similarly decorated and visited, and it may be that the well-dressings are a survival of ancient Nature-worship—of the old pagan practice of erecting altars and making sacrifices beside the wells and springs on which the people depended for what was indeed the water of life.

White Sunday

The Christian festival of Whitsun falls very often in May, Whit Sunday being the seventh Sunday after Easter ; the name means White Sunday, and it was applied because in olden days it was a favourite day for christenings, when white robes were worn. The festival commemorates the descent of the Holy Ghost on the Apostles assembled in Jerusalem after Christ's ascension, when they received the " gift of tongues," so that they might be able to preach the Gospel to foreign nations. The same day was the great Jewish feast of Pentecost.

Whitsuntide, like May-day and Easter, has many a link with the customs of our ancient, and pagan, forefathers. Indeed, we may say that for probably thousands of years this time of the year has been a period of merry-making and country sports and pastimes. Up to our grandfathers' time there used to be held what were called " Whitsun ales "— meetings of the chief people of the parish in some roomy barn near the church, where with one of the churchwardens in the chair, and with huge tankards of good old English ale on the table before them, they discussed local affairs and agreed on what repairs and improvements they should carry out in church and village during the coming year. In some places in England the local people used to perform the " Whitsun mysteries," i.e. plays of which the subjects were usually Adam and Eve in the Garden of Eden, Noah and his Ark, and other popular tales taken from the Bible. Then there were the Morris dancers.

Dancing with Maid Marian

" Morris " seems to come from " Morisco," the Spanish word for Moorish, and it is said that the Morris-dance was introduced into England from Spain, where there were then many Moors, by John of Gaunt in the fourteenth century. But the Moorish dancers, we are told, wore castanets or rattles at the end of their fingers, while the English morris-dancers had bells attached to various parts of their dress. The chief characters of the morris-dance were Robin Hood, Maid Marian, the hobby horse, and the jester or fool ; Maid Marian was dressed in a rich, brightly-coloured gown with a crown on her head, while Robin Hood was pictured as a bold and jolly outlaw, the lover of Maid Marian. But often the Morris-dance was performed by only one man or woman, and one of the most celebrated was William Kemp, a popular comic actor in the theatre of Queen Elizabeth's time. Once Kemp danced every step of the way from London to Norwich. Of the four weeks he took to do it, nine days were actually spent in dancing. Every now and again some man or girl would challenge him to a contest, to see who could outlast the other in dancing or jigging. There was one lusty country lass who said she was quite ready to dance a mile with him if he would lend her some of his bells. " I looked upon her," he says, " saw mirth in her eyes, heard

MORRIS DANCERS (*from an old print*)

boldness in her words, and beheld her ready to tuck up her russet petticoat. I fitted her with bells, which she, merrily taking, garnished her thick short legs with. The drum struck; forward marched I with my merry Maid Marian, who shook her fat sides and footed it merrily to Melford, being a long mile." There he parted from her, after having given her a " skinful of drink " and a crown (five-shilling piece) to buy some more. " For, good wench, she was in a piteous heat ; my kindness she requited with dropping some dozen of short courtesies, and bidding ' God bless the dancer.' I bade her adieu ; and, to give her her due, she danced truly."

Brides of May

On the Continent there are, or used to be, some even stranger Whitsun performances. In some places they used to play a sort of game in which a boy acted the part of a king and a little girl pretended to be his queen. In a village in Denmark a pretty little girl was dressed up in bride's finery, with a crown of spring flowers on her head ; the " bride-groom " was a boy just as gaily decorated. Then, with their little friends acting as their courtiers, they went in great state from farmhouse to farm-house, asking and receiving contributions of fresh eggs and butter, new loaves, cream, sugar, and candles. In some villages in Germany a girl dressed as the " May Bride " was similarly led about the countryside ; at every house at which the procession stopped she sang a song and asked for a present. If this was refused, she told the people of the house that since they had given her nothing, they would have nothing but ill-luck all the year through.

The girl and her followers would probably have been very surprised to learn that they were repeating a performance that, in the long, long ago, was supposed to make the seed in the ground grow into sturdy plants and give a bumper harvest. For the girl and boy were symbols of the spirits of vegetation, and their " marriage " was believed to influence, in some strange way, the actual seeds and plants.

Carrying Out Death

But there are also some grimmer Whitsuntide customs. Here in a German village they dress up a young fellow in leaves and moss; he hides in the wood, and when he is discovered, he is led away a prisoner, and his captors pretend to shoot him. After a time, however, they pick him up from where he has fallen, and, tying him on a cart, take him back to the village, were they tell everybody that they have caught the " Wild Man of the Wood."

If we cross the border into Czechoslovakia, we may see a band of young people, each wrapped in bark and carrying a wooden sword, leading prisoner a boy dressed like a king. At every farm they come to they pretend to chase the " King " from room to room, and then act as if they were cutting off his head. In another place in the same country the young people mount their horses, and again they put a lad dressed to represent a king in their midst. Then they give him a short start. He gallops off, and they follow at full speed. If he escapes, he is allowed to be " King " for another year; if they catch him, however, he is made to dismount, is whipped with hazel twigs, and—of course only in make-believe—his head is cut off.

Now we go to Italy, and join the crowd who are watching a huge stuffed figure of a man, which is seated in a chair on a big cart. Slowly the cart is dragged through the streets, the figure jerking up and down with every jolt. At length the figure is taken off the cart and laid on a pile of wood. Someone puts a match to the pile, and as the flames leap up, the people dance and sing. " What on earth does this mean ? " you ask. " Why," comes the reply, " we are burning the Carnival."

One more weird happening, this time in Germany again. You see those boys, carrying that " guy " made of straw ? If you follow them, you will find that they will make a bonfire of it just outside the village. They are " carrying out Death," you will be told. And here in another district there goes a procession of little girls, bearing a tiny coffin in which lies a doll ; when they come to the village well or to a river, they tip the coffin into the water. " We are carrying Death into the water," they sing.

What is the meaning of these extraordinary proceedings ? Who is supposed to be represented by the King who has his head cut off, by Carnival who is burnt, by Death who is drowned ?

Perhaps we shall learn the answer if we watch a little longer. Here in this village the children have taken their " guy," stripped him of his clothes and finery, and flung him into the water or torn him to pieces in the field. This done, they go into the wood, cut down a small fir-tree, peel off the bark, and then decorate it with garlands of evergreens, painted egg-shells, bright-coloured rags, and so on. The tree is now called " May " or " Summer," and boys carry it about from house to house. And as they go they sing :

> We have carried Death out,
> We are bringing the dear Summer back,
> The Summer and the May,
> And all the flowers gay.

So there is the explanation. The figures or

effigies that are treated so roughly are supposed to represent Winter that has just died—after which he comes to life again as Summer. All these queer customs have to do with that same fear that we read about some pages back in the chapter on March : the fear that Winter will never end and Summer

" CARRYING OUT WINTER " IN A CZECHOSLOVAK VILLAGE

never come. When they were begun, perhaps thousands of years ago, people really had that dread ; and they thought that by acting the death of Winter and the birth of Summer they would be doing something to bring about the real thing. The Whitsuntide customs are, in other words, examples of what is called " imitative magic " : if you want a thing very much indeed—in this case, the return of Spring and Summer after the long sleep of Winter—then you should *act* it, with the idea that Nature will then " take the tip."

But there is an even deeper meaning, and to get at this we must again turn to Sir J. G. Frazer's *Golden Bough*. That book, or series of books rather, opens with a grim scene that is described by Frazer in what is surely among the finest pieces of writing in modern English literature.

The King of the Wood

In one of Turner's magnificent paintings there is shown a little woodland lake, at Nemi, not far from Rome. " Diana's Mirror " it was called by the ancients, since it was believed that the beautiful goddess used to walk about its edge and admire herself in the still water. Beside the lake there was a temple dedicated to Diana. But in ancient times this lovely spot was the scene of a tragedy that happened not just once, but was repeated every year.

In this sacred grove (writes Frazer) there grew a certain tree round which at any time of the day, and probably far into the night, a grim figure might be seen to prowl. In his hand he carried a drawn sword, and he kept peering warily about him as if at every instant he expected to be set upon by an enemy. He was a priest and a murderer; and the man for whom he looked was sooner or later to murder him and hold the priesthood in his stead. Such was the rule of the sanctuary. A candidate for the priesthood could only succeed to office by slaying the priest, and having slain him, he retained office till he was himself slain by a stronger or a craftier.

The priest of Diana's temple at Nemi bore the title of " King of the Wood " and was supposed to be Diana's husband; and in the many, many pages of his great book Frazer tries to show that at the bottom of the murderous custom lay the belief that he personified the creative spirit or power of Nature. But being still a man, the time must come when he would grow old and die, in which case the spirit that was within him would be lost, with the most dire results to crops and herds, even to men and women. Nothing, no one, could then be born; everybody, everything, would eventually die. The right thing to do was obviously to see that the spirit was detached from the priest before he died, and the surest way to do this was to have the priest killed while he was yet hale and hearty, when—so it was firmly thought—the life-spirit that was within him (of which he was the incarnation) would be automatically transferred to the man who had conquered him by brute strength or by sheer cleverness. That dark figure beside the lake, then—the figure we might have seen if we had passed that way, perhaps on some wild night, with " the background of forest showing black and jagged against a lowering and stormy sky, the sighing of the wind in the branches, the rustle of the withered leaves under foot, the lapping of the cold water on the shore "—that " dark figure with a glitter of steel at the shoulder whenever the pale moon peers down at him through the matted boughs," was supposed to contain the Spirit of Life itself. When he grew weak and old, he was like Winter; when a new man, young and fresh and full of vigour, took his place, he was Spring come again. The old " King of the Wood " must be slain, and a new King take his place; otherwise men and plants and animals would lose the power of reproducing their kind.

Now let us turn to a very different subject.

Beating the Bounds

Some time in May fall what are called in the calendar of the Church of England the Rogation Days. They are the Monday, Tuesday, and Wednesday before Ascension Day, and the name comes from the fact that from very ancient times it has been the custom on those days for the clergyman and members of his congregation to perambulate or walk round the boundaries of his parish and to ask God's blessing (*rogare* is the Latin for " to ask ") on the fruits of the earth, and to give Him thanks for all the good things that He has provided. When England was a Roman Catholic country, the perambulation was enlivened by banners, lights, the ringing of hand-bells, and was accompanied by much feasting and general merry-making. At the Reformation in Henry VIII's time most of this was forbidden, but Queen Elizabeth ordered that, since the perambulation or walking-round was so useful—there were few maps in those days, and what there were, were so poor that it was an all-too-easy matter for a greedy landlord to steal a corner or a strip off a neighbour's field without anybody noticing it—it should be kept up as in olden days, but with not quite so much eating and drinking. At certain places the procession was to halt, and the clergyman was required to point out God's goodness and lead the people in singing a psalm of thanksgiving.

So on the Gange Days, as they were also called

(from the Old Saxon *gangen*, meaning "to go"), the vicar used to set out, accompanied by a crowd of men and women and all the small boys of the parish. Usually it was a merry ramble through all sorts of odd places. If a fence had been put up since the last visit, the "processioners" might break it down without any fear of being sued for damages. If a canal had been cut across the boundary, somebody had to strip and dive in. If a river or stream lay in the way, the people might walk through it if it were not too deep. If a house had been built on the boundary, then in they went at the door and out again through a window. High walls had to be climbed, a way had to be forced through thick woods, and at the corners or boundary-crosses small boys were whipped—not always lightly—or bumped head downwards. It was believed, no doubt rightly, that in being treated in this fashion, the younger generation would be likely to remember the places better. Sometimes a girl or young woman was bumped, much to her disgust. There are parishes in England with the same boundaries that they had in Anglo-Saxon times, before England had become one kingdom; and doubtless the yearly "gangings" had much to do with keeping those boundaries intact. Nor is the practice dead. In many places in England and Scotland the perambulation on the Rogation Days is still kept up, sometimes after it had been dropped for many years; and choir-boys and Boy Scouts are bumped or stood on their heads at the most important places on the boundary.

The custom has been Christian since the eighth

or ninth century, and as early as the fifth century a Christian bishop of Vienna adopted it at a time when earthquakes had wiped out many boundaries and worked havoc with the marks. Originally the custom arose in the days before Christianity; it is a continuation of the ancient Roman festivals of the Terminalia, held in honour of Terminus (we talk of a railway terminus!), who was the god of boundary stones put up between estates, and of the Ambarvalia, which was a solemn annual procession round the fields with the object of purifying them and making the crops grow. The former was held in February, the latter (like the perambulation on the Rogation Days) in May.

A very good description of the Ambarvalia is given by Walter Pater in his novel *Marius the Epicurean*, which tells of the life of a young Roman of some eighteen hundred years ago. There was no work done on that day. The spades and ploughs lay untouched, and were hung with wreaths of flowers. Master and servants went in solemn procession along the dry paths of vineyard and cornfield, taking with them the animals—cows and pigs and goats—that were to be sacrificed to the gods. As they went, the people, led by priests in strange stiff vestments and with ears of corn upon their heads, chanted hymns and prayers from an ancient scroll that was usually kept in the painted chest in the hall, with the family records. Early in the morning the girls of the farm had been busy filling large baskets with flowers of apple and cherry, to strew before the quaint images of Ceres, Bacchus, and other gods, as these in their little wooden houses were carried in the procession by white-clad youths. The altars in the fields were gay with garlands of wool and blossom and green herbs; and Marius, being a tender-hearted youth, could not help pitying the poor animals who, with looks of terror, approached the spot where they were doomed to be slaughtered.

As he lay in bed that night he turned his thoughts from that nasty piece of butcher's work to the little chapel in the room below, where stood the urns containing the ashes of his father and his ancestors. Daily from childhood had Marius taken them their share of the family meal, at the second course, amid the silence of the company. The dead genii, or spirits, were satisfied with so little, he reflected—a few violets, a cake dipped in wine, or a morsel of honeycomb. And thinking thus, he fell asleep.

Buddha's Birthday in Ceylon

Before we leave May, we should look for a moment at some Buddhist country—Ceylon, for instance— since it is in May, on the first full moon, that Buddhists hold their great festival of *Wesak*. This commemorates three events in the history of Buddha, the founder of the Buddhist faith. Buddha, it should be made quite clear, did not claim to be a god, even though in some countries that profess Buddhism he has come to be worshipped as such. He was a man who lived in the northern parts of India some five hundred years before Christ. The dates usually accepted for his birth and death are 563 and 483 B.C. respectively. It was on a day in May that he was born, the son of a " king," i.e. the rajah or ruler of a small principality. As a youth he was married to

Princess Yasodara, but at twenty-nine he left his lovely wife and new-born son and went out into the world as a penniless wanderer to see if he could discover the secret of existence. After six years of study and meditation and hardness of living, he was sitting beneath a tree in the forest when, after long and fierce temptations, he became " Enlightened "—that is what " Buddha " means. He learnt the Four Noble Truths, viz. the Truth of suffering, the existence of pain and ill ; the Truth that pain has a cause—thirst or craving or desire, that leads inevitably to re-birth after this life and innumerable further lives, in human or other forms ; the Truth that pain can be made to cease ; and the Truth that the way it can be made to cease is by following the Noble Eightfold Path, of which the steps are : right views, right intention, right speech, right action, right livelihood, right effort, right mindfulness, and right concentration. This also was on Buddha's birthday.

For over forty years Buddha wandered about from place to place, teaching the Truths that he had discovered, spending only the rainy season—that is, the period between May and October—in the monasteries that his followers established. Then, an old man of eighty, he died. But Buddhists prefer to say that he " attained Nirvana." What Nirvana is, none can say, since it is a state of being from which no one returns to this earth to tell ; but it is not " extinction," as many Western writers have declared. It was on his birthday that the great teacher passed to Nirvana.

These, then, are the important happenings that

JUGGERNAUT'S CAR DRAGGED THROUGH THE STREETS OF PURI
(*Topical Press*)

Buddhists recall and commemorate at *Wesak*. It is a time of much rejoicing. The houses are decorated, and before the statues of Buddha are placed offerings of flowers and choice and delicious fruits, which are afterwards partaken of by the priests or *bhikkhus*.

And here, to prevent another misunderstanding, it should be mentioned that the *bhikkhus* are not priests in the sense in which we use the word. They do not administer sacraments, nor do they offer sacrifices to the gods or to God. They are preachers, who live in monasteries and have to get their living by begging. It is a common sight in Ceylon and other Eastern lands to see them in their yellow robes and with shaven heads, moving from door to door, and holding out their wooden bowls in which the good and kind place their gifts. They are not importunate beggars. If anyone refuses them, they do not whine or snarl or swear, but move on to the next house and, without a word, again hold out the begging-bowl. But very few people do refuse, since it is a religious duty to give what one can afford to the men who, so it is believed, have chosen the holy way of life. It was the way of life that Buddha himself chose and followed ; and in the evenings, when it is dark, the Ceylonese sit out in the moonlight in little shanties of greenery and flowers, and listen with grave interest to the long sermons of the *bhikkhus*. The sermon is really a reading, and the favourite book is the *Jataka*, which contains hundreds of stories of Buddha, in his last life and in them any previous lives or incarnations that he is supposed to have had.

Many of these stories are older than Buddha's

time, and concern heroes—whether men or fairies or animals—who at first had no connection with him. Perhaps some of the tales were told round the camp-fires of the Aryan tribesfolk when they were still wandering about the great plains of central Asia, before they descended through the Himalayan passes into India, a thousand years and more before the opening of our Christian era.

The simple country people are not interested in the origin of the tales, however. They love the stories as stories, and they often spend the whole night in the open, dressed in their best clothes, chatting pleasantly with their neighbours as the *bhikkhu* now and again takes a rest, and chewing the betel leaves and areca nuts that are what pipes and cigarettes and sweets are with Westerners.

In many ways the Buddhism of today is very different from the Buddhism of the early centuries : Buddha would be greatly shocked if he could see some of the things that are done in his name. But the *Wesak* is Buddhism at its best and purest. At these festivals, it has been remarked, there is a spirit of human kindness that fits in admirably with the loveliness of the oriental night and scene, and with the gentle and loving teaching of Gautama, the Indian saint and seer who is styled the Buddha.

JUNE

LONG ages ago there was an Indian king named Indramena, who reigned over the country that is now Orissa, in north-eastern India. In spite of his wealth and greatness, he was very unhappy, for he had a guilty conscience. With alarm he realized that he had so far done nothing that would make it at all likely that when he died he would go to one of the many heavens in which Hindus believe. The thought made him miserable. He was used to rich and luxurious living; an army of soldiers were ready to do his bidding, while in his palace troops of the loveliest girls were proud and happy to be his servants. He shuddered when he thought that before long he might have to exchange this life of easy happiness for one in Naraka, the place of eternal darkness, where the only sounds are groans and lamentations, and in the blackness there creep all kinds of horrible creatures. So Indramena decided to ask his favourite god, Brahma with the Four Faces, what he should do in order to escape such a horrible fate.

The Temple beneath the Sands

Brahma with the Four Faces listened to him kindly. He could quite understand his anxiety. " Stop worrying, O King," he said, " I will find you a way out. Now listen carefully. Near the sea coast is a mountain called Nila, which is three leagues in length. This mountain is holy, because once a great god used to live there, and it had the power of taking away the burden of their sins from the people who came to worship in the temple of solid gold that was dedicated to Vishnu, my great brother god, and in olden days used to stand there. This temple still exists, but it has been completely buried by the sand cast up by the sea. If you want to make sure of going to heaven, seek out this buried temple and restore it to its ancient glory. You can be quite sure that if you renew the sacrifices that were formerly offered there to Vishnu, you will have nothing to fear."

The King was delighted with what he heard, and went on to ask Brahma just where the buried temple lay. " Ah, that I am sorry to say," replied the god, " I cannot tell you exactly. But not far from Nila you will find a tank, and in the tank lives a turtle as old as the world. He will be able to tell you far more than I can." Indramena bowed low in thanks, and then set off to find the tank.

That proved not at all difficult, and hardly had he arrived at the tank when a truly tremendous turtle waddled slowly up to him. Indramena introduced himself.

" Really, O Prince, I'm delighted to meet you," said the turtle, " and I should be highly delighted if I could be of any assistance. Unfortunately my great age has in some measure affected my memory. I can't recall things so easily as I used to do ; besides, I have lived so long that I have such a lot of things to remember. But it is quite true that there was once a golden temple, in which dwelt Vishnu, the

God of Gods, the God with Four Arms. But when the sand came up and buried it, he went away in a huff. For all that I know, the temple is still there, buried ever so deeply in the sand. But alas, I cannot remember just where it was. However, have a word with the crow which lives on the edge of the tank called Markandeya. He has been gifted with immortality, and he can recall everything that happened ages since."

So the King hastened to the tank Markandeya, and there sure enough was the crow. Once he had been glossy black like other crows, but he was now so extremely old that he had turned completely white.

" O crow," the King began, " who·enjoys the gift of immortality ! Do you remember that there was once a great king of this country who built a golden temple ? " " There certainly was," replied the crow ; " he was a very good king, and he built a magnificent temple. All the walls were of solid gold, and the inside was stuck all over with precious stones. And what is more, it still exists, absolutely unharmed, but beneath a huge mass of sand washed up by the sea. Nor has the Great God entirely deserted the place."

" Can you tell me where this wonderful palace lies buried ? " asked Indramena excitedly.

The crow beckoned him to follow, and after walking some little distance he began to peck vigorously at the sand. And lo and behold, he had not pecked more than a minute or two when he had uncovered what beyond the slightest doubt was a pinnacle of the golden temple. " There's where the temple lies buried," he said. Then with a few strokes of his beak he filled in the hole he had dug.

Going back to Brahma with the Four Faces, Indramena told him that he had succeeded in his quest; what was he to do now? Brahma told him that he must rebuild the temple—not of gold, however, but in stone. Then he must keep a careful watch on the seashore until a tree-trunk was washed up; that trunk would be in reality Krishna (the most popular and loved of all the Hindu gods, believed to be an *avatar* or incarnation of Vishnu), and the King must employ the famous carpenter Visvakarma to fashion it into a splendid image; then, with companion images of Subadra, the god's sister, and Balarama, his brother, it must be placed in the temple, and rich sacrifices offered before it.

Indramena carried out the instructions to the letter. Visvakarma arrived when he was summoned, and started work on the great image; he promised to finish it in one night, on the single condition that no one looked on while he was at work. But Indramena could not restrain his curiosity; he peeped through the cracks in the door, and was delighted to see that the carpenter was making excellent progress. But Visvakarma had seen him, and stopped work at once. So that is why the great image in the temple at Puri remains to this day little more than a tree-trunk.

That is the story of Jaganath (or Juggernaut, as the name became on English lips), the Lord of the Universe, as it is told by his priests to the crowds who come to worship at his shrine at Puri. Once a year, in June, the monster image is mounted on a huge carriage and dragged by devotees to the god's country house. It is a great festival, and immense crowds gather round the image and try to take a hand at the ropes. Travellers have described the extraordinary scenes that were witnessed before the crowds became regulated by soldiers and police.

One of those who saw the procession was the Portuguese friar Sebastião Manrique, who went to India in 1628 and wrote a book of " Travels " on his return home in 1645. Manrique describes the magnificence of Jaganath's temple, the rich offerings, the crowds of pilgrims, the excited mob as it sang and shouted in a frenzy of religious excitement. Then he goes on to tell that some of the pilgrims and the *yogis* or holy beggars, with the foam of madness on their lips, flung themselves beneath the massive wheels of the god's car and were crushed to death. Such was the manner of Juggernaut's progress. (And that is why we speak of a " Juggernaut " as something that moves on and over all who do not get out of its path.)

Strange Doings on Midsummer Eve

Of all the nights in the year, St. John's Eve or Midsummer Eve, the night before Midsummer Day (June 24), must surely be the most romantic. In country districts the village girls may still practise a kind of magic in order to discover who, if anybody, is going to fall in love with them in the coming year. Here are some of the things that they used to do. It was believed that if an unmarried girl, who had been careful not to eat any supper, laid the cloth at midnight with bread and cheese on the table, and then sat down, as if ready to eat, and with the door open—if she did this, then before the night was over the man she was to marry would come in, bow to her and drink her health, and then depart without a word. Another custom was for a girl to bake a special cake, and put a piece of it under her pillow; the young man would appear in her dreams. Yet another was to take a clean chemise, damp it, turn it inside out, and hang it over a chair; the

ST. JOHN'S WORT

sweetheart-to-be would come in and turn it the right way. Stalks of the orpine plant are still called "Midsummer men"; they are put into a flower-vase overnight, and if in the morning they bend towards one another, then it is a sure sign of a happy wedding. Another plant that enters into Midsummer magic is St. John's Wort; and in France, if not in England, it is often used for house decoration at this time of the year. Then if a girl goes out into the summer dusk, sows a patch of hemp-seed, and takes a quick peep over her shoulder—why, she will glimpse her future husband.

Some of these quaint old customs seem to have been based on the belief that on Midsummer Eve souls might leave the bodies of sleeping men and wander about at their own sweet will. But sometimes, so it was held, the wandering spirits did not make a love tryst; rather, they visited the places where during the coming year they were to die. So on

Midsummer Eve superstitious folk used to sit in the church porch and wait, shivering with cold and fright, to see the ghosts go past of people who were still in the land of the living. . . .

Watching at Stonehenge

Other watchings and waitings take place on this romantic night. In various parts of England there are hills and stone circles and other collections of

MIDSUMMER SUNRISE AT STONEHENGE

giant stones, put in place by the " ancient Britons " ages ago, which people make a point of visiting on Midsummer Eve, apparently in the belief that it will bring them good luck. Naturally enough, the most popular of such places is Stonehenge, Britain's oldest monument and the finest relic of the Stone Age that exists anywhere. Its origin is still something of a mystery, but it is popularly believed that it was used as a temple by the ancient Druids. It would certainly seem to have something to do with the worship of the sun, since the giant stones surround a flat stone —the so-called altar stone—on which the sun's rays fall directly on June 21—the day of the summer solstice, when the sun seems to turn about in the advancing course that it has followed since the other solstice in December. If the weather is fine, quite a thrill may be experienced by one who stands in the three-thousand-year-old circle and watches the sun's rays strike the outlying stone, known as the " Hele stone," which is directly in line with the " altar stone " and (on the other side of the circle) the stone that marks the midsummer sunset. Stonehenge has been called the " clock of the seasons," and so it may well have been. But some visitors who stand there waiting for the sun to rise across the Plain may think of other and dreadful scenes that those ancient stones have possibly witnessed. Is it a ·fact that Stonehenge was a Druids' Temple? If so, then we may imagine that we see on that " altar stone " a human sacrifice—some strapping young man, some beautiful girl—lying stretched out, tied down, unable to move. Around stand the white-robed priests, chanting their fierce hymns. Then as the first ray falls across the sacrifice, the head priest lifts high his stone knife and strikes. . . .

A grim enough picture, and unfortunately not an altogether improbable one. The accounts that have been handed down to us from Julius Caesar and other Roman writers who had actual contact with our remote ancestors, contain many a reference to the horrible practices that accompanied the religion of the ancient Britons. Thus they are said to have enclosed men and women in huge structures of wicker-work, which they then set on fire.

Bonfires in the June Night

Midsummer used to be a favourite time for lighting bonfires, as popular as the beginning of November. In most of the countries, and even in the Mohammedan lands of North Africa, fires were (and in many places still are) lighted on hills and mountains, so that the night presented a wonderful spectacle. A Bohemian girl who sees nine bonfires at once is sure of a husband. In many places the people used to leap through the flames, or drive their animals through them, believing that this was a cure for sickness and a preventative of future ill. In Greece the peasants delight to leap through the flames of the Midsummer fires, but they say it is because they are tired of the fleas. In some places, including the Vale of Glamorgan in Wales, the countryfolk used to wrap a cart-wheel in straw, set it on fire, and then let it roll down the hill; if it kept blazing all the way down and for some little time afterwards, it was a sign of a bumper harvest. In just the same way, the people of a village in the valley of the Moselle in western Germany used to set fire to a straw-wrapped wheel, which the young men trundled down the hill into the river; if it was still burning and sizzled in the water, a fine vintage or wine harvest might be confidently expected.

Sun Worship in the Land of the Incas

Now we visit Peru, the Land of the Incas, in the days not long before the arrival of the Spanish *conquistadores.* In Cuzco, the capital city of the vast empire on the South American plateau, there stands the magnificent temple of the Sun-God—the " Place of Gold " it is styled, and very properly so, since the whole interior is a mass of gold. Walls and ceiling are encrusted with golden ornaments, and on one wall glitters a representation of the Sun-God— a human face engraved on a plate of solid gold of massive dimensions, thickly powdered with emeralds and other precious stones. Within the temple stands the altar on which burns the fire that is the emblem of the Sun; it is carefully tended by a band of high-born and highly-educated and very beautiful maidens—the " Virgins of the Sun," they are styled, or the " Elect "—whose chief duty is to see that the flame does not go out. If by any chance it does expire, that is considered to be a very bad omen indeed, and woe to the unfortunate priestess whose neglect has permitted the tragedy! She will certainly be expelled from the temple, and may be buried alive.

In this splendid building are celebrated the national festivals of the Incas and their people, and of these none are more impressive, more solemn, than the festivals that are held every year at the time of the solstices—round about our June 21 and December 22. It is then that the sun, having touched the northern or the southern extremity of his course, begins to retrace his steps as if to gladden the hearts of his chosen people by his presence. It is one of these festivals that we are privileged to attend.

The scene is described by the American historian, W. H. Prescott, in his *History of the Conquest of Peru.*

For three days the people have been fasting, and no fire has been permitted in their dwellings. Now at dawn the Inca, or Emperor, with his court, followed by the whole population of the city, have assembled in the great square of Cuzco to greet the rising of the Sun. They are dressed in their gayest apparel, and the Indian lords vie with each other in the display of costly ornaments and jewels on their persons, while canopies of gaudy feather-work and richly-tinted stuffs, borne by the attendants over their heads, give to the great square and the streets that empty into it the appearance of being spread over with one vast and magnificent awning. Eagerly the crowd watch for the coming of their deity; and no sooner do the first yellow rays strike the loftiest turrets than a great shout of welcome breaks out, accompanied by songs of triumph and the wild melody of barbaric instruments, that swells and swells as the bright orb, rising higher and higher above the mountains to the east, shines in full splendour on his worshippers. All bow in homage and prayer; then the Inca drinks from a huge golden vase, filled with the fermented liquor of maize, and invites his attendants to do likewise, in honour of the great god who has not forgotten to return.

Now sacrifices are offered—of llamas, grain, flowers, and sweet-scented gums, but sometimes (though not so often as in Aztec Mexico) of a child or a beautiful maiden. The priests peer and poke in the inside of the llamas to see if the signs are fortunate or otherwise, just as did the Augurs fifteen hundred years before in ancient Rome. Then a fire is kindled by means of a concave mirror of polished metal, which collects the rays of the Sun into a focus upon a heap of dried cotton and sets it alight. (This, too, was the method used in ancient Rome on similar occasions.) If the sky is overcast—which is considered to be a bad omen—the sacred fire is obtained by friction, rubbing together two pieces of wood.

Now the Sun has come back, the fire has been lit. It is a time for feasting and rejoicing. The sacrificed animals are cut up and distributed among the congregation. The Inca seats himself at the royal board with his courtiers, and eats of the meat and of a special bread made by the fair hands of the Virgins of the Sun. The Inca rises and toasts his people in generous goblets of fermented liquor, and as darkness falls the long revelry of the day is terminated by music and dancing. This goes on for several days, so pleased are the people—and so relieved—at knowing that for another period their great Sun-God will not desert them.

So we could go on, collecting examples of these Midsummer fires from here, there, almost everywhere. Probably all have had very much the same origin. The summer solstice is a great turning-point in the Sun's career, and to know " what he would do next " must have been a matter of the most painful concern to primitive men. The Peruvians welcomed his return, but in these northern latitudes what the people feared was that the Sun would never come back. And if he went away, what would happen to poor humanity? What was to prevent the flame of the torch (which was the only means of artificial light in those days) from doing the same thing? A world of perpetual night, of darkness without end : man must have found the idea horribly oppressive, hardly to be thought about. So he practised magic. He lit bonfires to stimulate the Sun's flagging energies, and made fiery wheels that whirled round and round as if to encourage the Sun to " keep on turning " in the sky.

JULY

"THEN came hot July, boiling like to fire," wrote Spenser. "That all his garments he had cast away. . . ." Well, it is not always like that. Some Julys, in this country of all-too-uncertain weather, are wet and cold and miserable. But according to the poets, it is the height of " sweet summer-time," when the Sun shines brightly from early morn until late evening, so that it is still " light enough to see " at ten o'clock.

It was given its name, we are told, by Mark Antony, who wished to do honour to his friend Julius Caesar, who had fallen beneath Brutus's dagger ; he chose it because it is the month when the Sun is generally most powerful, and therefore best suited to commemorate one who had been in fact the emperor of the Western World and therefore fully deserved to be the leader of half the year.

The Romans, it is interesting to note, believed that in some way this hot season of the year was under the special influence of the " Dog star," as they called Sirius, and that is why to this day the period from July 3 to August 11 is called the Dog-days. For many centuries our ancestors thought that at this time, presumably because of the heat, dogs were particularly liable to fits of bad temper or to go mad and bite people ; for this reason the magistrates used to order that all dogs should be muzzled about the beginning of July.

HARVEST HOME A HUNDRED YEARS AGO

(Reproduced, together with several other illustrations in this work, from
Robert Chambers's *Book of Days*, by kind permission of the publishers,
Messrs. W. & R. Chambers, Ltd.)

A New Robe for Athene

It was in July that the ancient Greeks used to celebrate in Athens, every four years, the great festival of the Panathenaea—the festival of Athene, the patron goddess of the city. In the days of Pericles, about the middle of the fifth century B.C., this was the occasion for feasting and rejoicing, competitions between the most skilled and handsome athletes and gymnasts, and magnificent processions in which the " Maiden Goddess " was honoured at the same time as the glorious history of the city was recalled. On the first day musical and literary competitions were held in the Odeum, as the chief theatre was called, and passages from Homer's poems were recited by the best elocutionists. Gymnastic sports of every kind followed for two days. Boys, youths, and men ran races, jumped, wrestled, threw the discus, and so on ; on the third night there was held what was probably the most popular of all the spectacles—a relay race in which the naked runners swept through the dark with flaming torches held high in their hands. The winners of all these events received jars filled with olive oil, and some of these jars, beautifully designed and painted with scenes from old Greek legends, have been preserved. The next day—the fourth— was given up to chariot-racing—another most exciting sport—and to exhibitions of fine horsemanship. In the evening there were races at sea along the coast by armed ships, and the beaches were crowded by the supporters of the rival vessels, who cheered themselves hoarse as their favourites went

by, making a great splashing with their oars.   Then
perhaps there was a beauty contest—not of girls,
however, but of young men, for in Athens the respectable women and girls, at least of the well-to-do
classes, were hardly ever allowed out of doors.

At last the morning of the sixth day dawns.   In a
big open space near one of the city gates preparations
are on foot for the largest and finest procession, in
which is to be carried a fine new robe for the statue
of Athenè in the Parthenon, the " Maiden's House "
on the flat summit of the Acropolis.

Most fortunately we can see for ourselves just what
the procession looked like, since it is represented in

" CARRYING TRAYS OF GIFTS AND JARS OF WINE "
(*Illustrations on these two pages from the*

"COWS TO BE SACRIFICED ON THE ALTAR"

the splendid sculptures—still vividly real after more than two thousand years of exposure to the weather and bad treatment—that used to form part of the frieze of the Parthenon, and a great part of which is among the most treasured exhibits of the British Museum in London.

The subject chosen by Pheidias, most famous of ancient sculptors, for his frieze is, then, the Panathenaic procession. We see the chief gods and goddesses sitting together to watch the start. Next we note a number of young knights just about to mount their horses, and some who have already done so. Then the cavalcade moves off. At the very

"CHARIOTS DRAWN BY PRANCING HORSES"
Acropolis frieze in the British Museum)
107

front goes the new robe, hung like a sail on a ship mounted on wheels. Then come the cows and sheep that are to be sacrificed on the altar, and next a band of musicians, playing lyres and flutes, and youths and maidens carrying trays of gifts and jars of wine. Several chariots follow, each drawn by prancing horses, and finally the gallant young riders on their spirited steeds. Amid cheering crowds the procession moves slowly through the market-place and arrives in the open space before the Acropolis. Here the riders dismount, and all move up the steps to the temple, and take their places in front of the great bronze statue of Athene, where Pericles and his chief officers are already grouped. Then, as the animal sacrifices are slaughtered on the altar, the robe is carried by the priests into the shrine and draped with solemn care over the statue's shoulders. From the top of the steps a herald steps out, and shouts in a voice that everyone can hear, that the Maiden, the city's own particular goddess has been good enough to accept the gift of her loyal subjects. This closes the official proceedings. The citizens stream away, and spend the rest of the day in feasting and merry-making. For tonight the holiday ends, and tomorrow all must be at work again.

Such is the scene that Pheidias and his assistant artists have pictured with unrivalled grace and vigour, so that the sunny July day of so many centuries ago seems to come to life before our eyes.

A Party on Pasali-day

In India the month that overlaps the end of our July and the beginning of August is the most sacred of all the months of the year for the followers of the great god Siva. Indian girls think that it is an unlucky month for weddings, even more so than English girls think the same thing of May. But some very interesting ceremonies take place in Sravana, this tenth month of the Indian year.

Thus the first Sunday in the month is Pasali-day; the word means in one of the Indian languages the palm of the hand. On this day brothers and sisters are even more affectionate than usual. The grown-up brothers (who are, of course, usually married) invite their young unmarried sisters to their homes, where they feast on a specially prepared dish of wheat, treacle, and clarified butter, and the girls are given presents of money, pieces of cloth, or a pretty bodice. In the course of the day, the sister, or one of the sisters, draws on a leaf of the pipal tree a picture of the goddess who is Siva's wife, and puts it on a little table with another leaf on which she arranges a thread for each brother, while on a third she puts a little piece of the special dish they have just enjoyed : this is intended as a gift for the goddess, and brothers and sisters join in worship. But some girls are so unfortunate as not to have any brother ; in this case they make a solemn promise that if the goddess will send them a baby brother, then on every Pasali-day they will eat only just as much as will fill the baby's tiny palms.

A few days later in the month, the goddess of smallpox may, be specially remembered—not gratefully, of course, but in the hope that she will be so pleased at the attention that she will not attack anyone with her dreaded and dreadful disease. Then come four days of a great fair, which the children enjoy, it need hardly be said, as much as anybody and more than most people. In some parts of India one of the fair days is kept as Krishna's birthday, and about ten o'clock at night everybody, young and old, goes to the temple and listens to the story of the birth of this favourite god of the Hindu people.

Krishna's Birthday

Krishna, as we have already noted, is Vishnu under another name, or, to put it more precisely, he is supposed to have been the eighth of the *avatars*, or incarnations, of the great god. According to the old legend, Vishnu plucked out two of his own hairs, a white one and a black; the black one became Krishna—whose name means " the Black "—and the other became his brother Balarama. Krishna is supposed to have been born in a stable, and the chief moment of the service I have just mentioned is when at midnight the doors of the inner shrine of the temple are thrown open, to reveal an image of the infant Krishna lying in a cradle. (Whereupon the people offer gifts of money, spices, coconuts, and so on, and watch the image as it is carefully bathed by a priest.) A wicked uncle plotted to kill Krishna out of jealousy, but the child had been smuggled away for safety to a cowherd's hut, where he spent the happy years of childhood. He grew up to be a very jolly youth, much given to playing practical jokes. He used to run off with the milk and butter, which he shared among his playmates and the shepherdesses and milkmaids.

Once when the girls were bathing, he stole their clothes and hid up a tree, so that they were a long time in finding where he was. Often he played the flute, and he became a very good dancer. He was so handsome that all the maidens fell in love with him, and he married seven or eight of them. Once on one of his rambles he met a crooked girl, and because she was kind to him he made her as straight as a young tree. He fought and killed in single combat many a giant and ogre. He put the demons to flight. He married a great many wives, and had so many sons that they could not be counted at all accurately. At length he died, whether in battle or whether by accident when out hunting is not clear. An immense number of stories, not all of them pleasant, are told of the jovial young god, and he is a principal figure in the *Bhagavad Gita*, the " Song of the Divine One," which is a section of that vast epic—probably it is the longest poem in the world, since it contains about 220,000 lines—called the *Mahabharata*.

A Kiss for the Cow

On yet another day in this same month, Indian women of the higher castes worship the cow. In the temple courtyard a cow is tethered, with perhaps her calf beside her. While the women sit watching in reverent silence, the priest bathes the cow's hooves, places a red-coloured thread on her horns, and makes offerings of flowers, moistened wheat, incense, and so on. Then the women move round the cow four times, and each time they pour water on her tail out of the jug that they carry, and lift the wet tip to their eyes and head. Finally, each kisses the patient beast, and whispers into her right ear that " Truth belongs to you, and it is our duty to keep our promises."

The cow, it should be remarked, is a sacred animal to all Hindus. To kill a cow is one of the worst of sins, in the religious sense ; cow-murder used to be punished with death. It is forbidden to put a cow out of her misery, even when she is so old and rotted with disease that movement is next to impossible. Why this should be so is not satisfactorily explained ; but beyond a doubt the cow is the most useful animal in India, since it provides milk and butter, and the dung that is practically the only fuel. But those millions of Indians who are not Hindus—who do not practise the religion of Hinduism but belong to the great rival religion of Islam or Mohammedanism—take a very different view. To them the cow is valuable as a source of beef. So, as it has been asked, how can there be peace between the members of the two religions, when in one religion the cow is worshipped and in the other the cow is eaten ? This is one of the main causes of strife in present-day India ; and so bitter is the feeling aroused, that in 1947 Indian statesmen agreed that the only thing to do was to divide their country into two Dominions. So there were established two countries in the Indian peninsula where under the British there had been only one. In one, Pakistan, the Moslem or Mohammedan state, the cow is eaten, and most people think that that is a natural and perfectly right and proper thing to do. In the other, however, in the Dominion of India, the killing of a cow is likely to give rise to a tremendous outcry, since it is considered to be a sin, even a crime, which is absolutely forbidden by the religion that the great majority of the people profess.

If by about the middle of Sravana the monsoon rains have not begun, the Hindu people become exceedingly anxious, fearing a failure of the harvests and consequent famine. The Brahmans, the priest-scholars, go to the temples of Siva (who is worshipped as the Destroyer, while Brahma is worshipped as the Creator and Vishnu as the Preserver), and pour water over his emblem, in the hope of putting him in a good humour and making him realize what deadly peril he has brought upon the people by holding up the rains.

But in England, too, July is the month when rain should fall—or should not fall. For July 15 is St. Swithin's Day.

If it Rains on St. Swithin's

Swithun or Swithin was a monk of the Abbey of Winchester, who in course of time became the trusted adviser and minister of the King. In 852 he was appointed bishop of Winchester, and about ten years later he died, giving instructions that he should be buried in the churchyard, beside the north wall of the church, so that the water from the eaves would drip on his grave. There for a hundred years and more his body rested. Then there were stories of strange happenings at the grave. A deformed man had been relieved of his hump in a twinkling, another had prayed beside the grave and had been cured of grievous eye trouble. These wonderful events were reported to King Edgar, and he gave orders that Swithun's remains should be dug up and placed in a magnificent tomb in the great abbey church. This was done on July 15, 971.

ST. SWITHIN'S STATUE AT WINCHESTER

It would seem that in the earliest accounts of the ceremony there is no mention of any rain; on the contrary, the day is said to have been fine, and the translation of the saint's bones was accomplished without any trouble. But the popular story—which is probably much later, and owes something to some old pagan legend—has it that just as the ceremony was about to begin it started to rain, and the rain continued without a break for the forty succeeding days. In whatever way the belief arose, it is one of the commonest sayings that—

St. Swithin's Day, if thou dost rain,
For forty days it will remain :
St. Swithin's Day, if thou be fair,
For forty days 'twill rain no more.

In France a similar belief is associated with St.

Médard, but *his* " day " is June 8. It arose, so runs the story, on a very hot day in summer, when suddenly there was a terrific storm. Everybody who was out of doors got drenched—everybody save St. Médard, since an eagle flapped his wings over the saint's head and so kept the rain off. In Belgium, Germany, and other countries there are also " rainy saints ".

Keeping the Great Fast of Ramadan

Owing to the arrangement of the calendar of the Moslems or Mohammedans, it happens sometimes (it is happening in these middle years of the twentieth century) that the month of Ramadan—the month of the great fast—falls at the height of summer, when it must seem all the harder to observe its strict requirements. Between one new moon and the next all good Moslems must abstain from eating and drinking from daybreak until it is too dark to be able to distinguish a white thread from a black. Nothing whatever must enter their mouths. Even injections are forbidden. Smoking is banned. So, too, are refreshing scents and baths. Some particularly strict Moslems try their hardest not to swallow their saliva, and not to open their mouths wider than ordinarily so as to draw in an extra large mouthful of fresh air. There must be no kissing. But as soon as it is really dark, then eating and drinking are allowed, until day comes again. Mohammedanism or Islam is very human in some of its laws, however, and it is specially provided that some people may be excused the Ramadan fast; for instance, travellers, the very sick, mothers with

115

babies in arms, young children, and aged folk. If Ramadan falls in the summer, when nights are short, the fast may be for nearly sixteen hours ; but if the month falls in winter, it may be about twelve hours.

As soon as the last night of Ramadan has come to an end, there begins a period of great rejoicing— what is called the Greater Bairam, or the Festival of the Breaking of the Fast. Soon after sunrise the people dress in new, or at least their best, clothes— everyone tries to wear something new, even if only a pair of shoes—and men go to service in the mosques. Friends meeting in the street embrace and kiss each other. Servants are given small presents. Special dishes are cooked at home, or meals are taken in restaurants. The streets are gay with joyful people dressed in holiday finery.

But on at least one day of the festival members of most families, particularly the women, are in the habit of paying a visit to the tombs of their relatives and friends. They carry branches of palm and bunches of sweet basil to lay on the graves. Sometimes they pitch little tents in the cemeteries, over the grave they have come to visit, and there they spend the heat of the day, or they may stay there for a night or two. In some places this tomb-visiting has its lighter side, since travelling showmen set up their swings and roundabouts at the cemetery gates, and draw big crowds of spectators.

AUGUST

AUGUST—the month of the year's most popular Bank Holiday, the month when the schools have " broken up " and the parks and seaside beaches are thronged with young people enjoying themselves after the strenuous and nerve-wracking time of examinations at the end of the school year. With many other peoples the month is one of holiday and relaxation. With the Buddhists of Ceylon, for instance, it is the month when the great festival of the Perahera is celebrated.

This is the festival of carrying the " Sacred Tooth," and it takes place at Kandy, in the centre of the island. The Tooth is supposed to be one of Buddha's, and it has a most interesting history. According to the story, it was brought to Ceylon in A.D. 311 in the hair of an Indian princess, and lodged in a temple at Anuradhapura. Immediately it was regarded as the island's most precious possession, and the King of Lanka, the local sovereign, valued it as the supreme symbol of his authority. Once or twice it was stolen, but it was recovered and put back in its shrine. Then in 1560 a terrible thing happened. The Tooth was captured by the Portuguese, and carried away in triumph to their stronghold of Goa on the coast of India.

At first there was some talk of letting it be ransomed, but the Archbishop of Goa would have nothing to do with such a proposal. He was an exceedingly devoted Roman Catholic, and to him the Tooth was nothing more or less than a heathen idol. So he arranged a great public ceremony, and before a huge crowd of Europeans and Indians he placed the Tooth in a mortar, ground it to powder, burnt the dust in a brazier, and then threw what was left into the sea.

One would have thought that that would have been the end of Buddha's Tooth. But it was not so. A few years after its public destruction the Tooth mysteriously reappeared at Kandy, where since 1566 it has been housed in the inner shrine of the Temple of the Tooth. Only the most exalted and favoured visitors are allowed to see the Tooth, which is enshrined in seven caskets, fitting neatly into each other ; those who have been privileged to see it have said that it is nearly three inches in height and about the thickness of a man's little finger. If this be so, then obviously it can never have come from Buddha's mouth, or from the mouth of any human being. Perhaps—it is suggested—it originally formed part of the eating apparatus of some prehistoric monster. At least, say the sceptics, the monks of Kandy might have taken the trouble to obtain a human tooth to replace the one that they had lost !

The Buddhists of Ceylon, however, have no doubts about the authenticity of their sacred relic. They allege that the Tooth was never really stolen, but that it has remained in Ceylon all the time. Fortunately we have not to decide what would seem to be an exceedingly tricky matter. The Tooth is there, wherever it came from in the first place ;

and every August the precious nest of caskets containing it is taken in procession through the streets
of Kandy, carried on the richly-caparisoned back
of a fine elephant. In front stride the chieftains of
the place, dressed in gorgeous silken robes and high,

THE PROCESSION OF THE SACRED TOOTH IN CEYLON

bejewelled hats, and carrying huge silk umbrellas.
Round the city they go, and when the shrine is
again reached there is a performance of the sacred
dance. To the music of cymbals and drums rows of
young men move slowly forward and then back, turn
round, stretch their arms and hands, whirl and jump
as the music gathers speed and force, and finally

burst out into a long-drawn-out religious song or hymn. Every night for ten days the procession is repeated, and the people get more and more excited. Sometimes as many as a hundred splendid elephants take part in the procession, and the performances of the " devil dancers " meets with the rapturous applause that it richly deserves.

Just a Pinch of Incense

Like July, August reminds us of a great Roman. The name was given to it by Augustus, the great-nephew and successor of Julius Caesar in the head-ship of the Roman realm, and he chose to do so because a number of lucky things had happened to him in the month. In the old calendar it had had only twenty-six days. Julius Caesar decreed that it should have thirty, and when Augustus gave it his name he took a day from February and tacked it on to August, since it was not to be thought of that *his* month should have fewer days than any of the others.

Augustus was the first of the Roman emperors, and it was during his reign that the practice of emperor-worship began. It was taught that the Emperor for the time being was quite as good as a god; indeed, he was a god, and before his bust, placed in the public squares and town halls, every good citizen was expected to bow respectfully and offer a pinch of incense in reverential homage to the head of the State, the lofty being who symbolized the Roman country and people. When Christianity arose, this practice caused much distress to the members of the new religion. They felt that religious homage was due to God alone, and that their consciences did not permit them to offer the customary pinch of incense. Their pagan neighbours found this reluctance very hard to understand. " Surely," they said, " you can have no objection to paying so small a mark of respect to the Emperor, who stands for all that is good and great in the Roman world ? " The Christians thought otherwise, however, and many of them paid the penalty of their refusal to do as their neighbours did. They were exposed to fines and imprisonment, and some were put to death in horrible fashion. Not until Christianity became the official religion of the Empire, early in the fourth century, were they finally exempted from complying with pagan customs and ceremonies.

The early Christians refused to " bow the knee to Caesar," as the saying went, because to do so was regarded by them as an act of disloyalty to the Lord Jesus. But, as we have seen, and shall see again when we come to consider the Christmas festival, there were many pagan ways that were not looked upon as being altogether objectionable. Whenever they could do so, the Christian bishops and missionaries, being wise folk, decided to make it as easy as possible for the convert. If he had been used to enjoy a festival at a certain period of the year, then let him enjoy it still ; but let him understand that now it is held in honour not of the pagan gods —who, so the Christians believed, actually existed, though not as gods but as devils—but of the One True God. So we may suppose the argument to have run.

The First Sheaf at Lammastide

At the very beginning of August we have an instance of a pagan occasion that has been " converted." The 1st of August is called in the Church calendar Lammas ; this word, we are told, comes from the old English *Hlafmaesse* (loaf mass), a loaf made of the first new corn being the usual offering at Mass on that day. There is evidence that this festival of thanksgiving for another harvest safely come to the reaping goes back long, long before Christianity was first preached. After all, it is a natural custom, such as primitive man may well have observed ever since it was first discovered that by putting certain seeds in the ground, and leaving them there to grow, you may expect to receive fifty or a hundred times what you sowed. He thought it only right and proper that he should make a display of good cheer and good will, and give thanks to the god or gods who had granted him this immense boon of relief from the fear and threat of starvation.

The old Celtic peoples of Britain and Western Europe celebrated on August 1 their festival of Lugnasadh, named after a god Lug or Lugus, who seems to have been the patron not only of early harvests but horse-racing and marriages.

The " harvest home," of which the Lammas festivities were the first instalment, as it were, has always been marked by feasting and jollity, and it still is in those country districts where there is a love and respect for the old ways. Still one may see set up in or over the farm-house a straw symbol or image of the " corn spirit "—a bunch of cornstalks with the grain in full ear. At Ackworth, near Pontefract, in Yorkshire, the rector cuts the first sheaf, and then hangs it on the effigy of St. Cuthbert over the church porch, just as the Norsemen of a thousand years ago used to hang up a similar sheaf as provender for the ravens of Odin, greatest and best loved of their gods. The eating and drinking, the singing and dancing, that go to make up the harvest celebration are relics, there can be no doubt, of the old-time adoration of the divine bestower of health, wealth, and happiness. The clergyman at Ackworth is doing what the Norsemen did before they became Christians.

In many other parts of England and Scotland there are similar reminders of the one-time gods and goddesses whom our forefathers worshipped. The actual names they went by have been forgotten; probably the Christian missionaries insisted that these should be taboo, even though the old customs might be retained. In a district in Kent the harvest spirit is known as the " ivy girl," in Derbyshire she is the " maiden," in Shropshire and Hertfordshire the " mare." In Scotland she may be called the " maiden," the " old wife," the " Kern baby " or the " Kern doll." Elsewhere it is a " he," referred to as the " Old Man."

The Ballad of John Barleycorn

The songs sung at the " harvest homes " may also take us back to the days of paganism. There is a famous ballad by Robert Burns in praise of John Barleycorn that may be taken as indicating the real origin of the belief in the Corn Spirit. " Three kings," we are told at the beginning, " hae sworn a solemn oath John Barleycorn should die."

> They took a plough, and plough'd him down,
>   Put clods upon his head,
> And they hae sworn a solemn oath
>   John Barleycorn was dead.
>
> But the cheerful Spring came kindly on,
>   And show'rs began to fall ;
> John Barleycorn got up again,
>   And sore surpris'd them all.
>
> The sultry suns of Summer came,
>   And he grew thick and strong ;
> His head well arm'd wi' pointed spears,
>   That no one should him wrong.
>
> The sober Autumn enter'd mild,
>   When he grew wan and pale ;
> His bending joints and drooping head
>   Show'd he began to fail.
>
> His colour sicken'd more and more,
>   He faded into age ;
> And then his enemies began
>   To show their deadly rage.

They have taken a scythe, long and sharp, the ballad goes on, and cut him by the knee ; they have tied him upon a cart, and then " laid him down upon his back and cudgell'd him full sore "—a reference to the operation of thrashing the corn with a flail. Then they dropped John Barleycorn into water and " let him sink or swim." Next they " laid him out upon the floor, to work him further woe," and " toss'd him to and fro " :

> They wasted, o'er a scorching flame,
>   The marrow of his bones ;
> But a miller us'd him worst of all,
>   For he crush'd him between two stones.

And they hae taen his very heart's blood
  And drank it round and round;
And still the more and more they drank,
  Their joy did more abound.

John Barleycorn was a hero bold,
  Of noble enterprise;
For if you do but taste his blood,
  'Twill make your courage rise.

So runs the drinking-song that Burns wrote, or adapted from some ancient original. Maybe a version had been sung by the Scottish peasants in the days of paganism. Indeed, it is very likely that the ballad arose in circumstances very different from the jovial carousals that Burns was so fond of. It has been suggested that this old song is a fragment of ancient mythology, telling of the slaying of the Corn Spirit—John Barleycorn—who, however, sprang up again in the spring to provide mankind with food and drink.

Already we have encountered some such idea as this in the story of Demeter and Persephone. That is a beautiful story, telling of a mother's love and determination to rescue her daughter from a gloomy fate. *John Barleycorn* introduces us, however, to the grimmer side of the old pagan belief.

The Tragedy of the Corn Spirit

Sir James Frazer refers to a song that was sung by the harvesters at reaping and threshing in Phrygia, a country of ancient times in what is now Asia Minor. This song was about one Lityerses, the son of the local king, who used to reap the corn, and compel any stranger who happened to be passing to join him in the labour. Then, when he was not looking, he would slay him, cut off his head with his sickle, and carry away his body wrapped in a sheaf. At last he more than met his match. Hercules came one day to help him in the reaping; and at the end, although someone died, it was not Hercules. The Greek hero cut off Lityerses' head with his sickle, and threw his corpse into the river. There are reasons for believing, says Frazer, that this story of Lityerses describes a real harvest custom among the Phrygians of old. Certain persons, especially strangers passing the harvest-field, were considered to be embodiments of the corn spirit, and as such were surprised and seized by the reapers, wrapped in sheaves and beheaded, after which their bodies were thrown into the water—presumably as a charm intended to produce rain.

This suggestion is supported by harvest customs in many parts of Europe that have lasted into our own time. Cases have been reported of European reapers who have pounced on a passing stranger and tied him up in sheaf; they have not killed him, but by word and gesture they have shown a pretty strong inclination to do so. In the district of Mecklenburg, in Germany, if the master or the mistress or a stranger enters the field where the mowers are busy on the first day of harvest, the latter turn towards the newcomer, make a great show of sharpening their scythes, and demand a forfeit by way of ransom. In one part of Lorraine the reapers shout in unison, as they are clearing the last corner of the field, " We are killing the Old Woman! We are killing the Old Woman!". Coming nearer home, there is, or was, a custom in the East Riding of Yorkshire of setting light to the last sheaf as a heap of stubble ; this is called " burning the Old Witch." Sometimes a man lies down on the threshing-floor and the last sheaves are thrashed on his body, or the farmer's wife is thrust with the last sheaf under the threshing-machine as if she is to be threshed. Such customs are very widespread, in Asia and Africa as well as in Europe, and they all seem to be based on the idea that the spirit of the corn is contained in the last sheaf, or in the person who cuts, binds, or threshes the last sheaf ; and the little piece of make-believe—the wrapping in a sheaf, the slaying or the thrashing—is a very much watered-down survival of an ancient custom. In modern times the procedure is just a game, a bit of sport. But in the old days there was nothing playful about it. The victim really was captured and put to death.

If we ask " why ? ", the answer would seem to be that the man was sacrificed as the embodiment of the Corn Spirit. Among many primitive or savage peoples, up to a time not long ago, it was the practice, when they sowed in the fields and when they reaped what they had sown, to make human sacrifices to the gods. Such was the practice of the Mexican Indians and certain of the Red Indians tribes who used to roam the American prairies, of the inhabitants of the jungles of West Africa and the islands of the Philippines, of the villagers in Bengal and other parts of India. Usually when the victim had been slain his blood was drunk or his flesh was eaten ; in so doing the worshippers believed that they were partaking of the body and blood of their god. The meal was a sacrament which could not fail to be of the greatest benefit to those who shared in it; unless the Corn Spirit were periodically embodied, captured, slain, and eaten, there would be a halt in the procession of the seasons—the rain would not fall, the sun would refuse to shine, the gladsome period of the harvest would be slow in coming, perhaps it would not come at all.

John Barleycorn, then, whose body was killed and threshed, whose heart's blood was drunk, may well have been originally a victim such as we read about in the Lityerses story, who was regarded as the embodiment of the Corn Spirit who must die in order that he might be re-born in fresh and more vigorous life.

Poor Little Maize Goddess !

If we move across the world and back through a matter of four or five hundred years to the Mexico of the Aztecs—the people who, originally invaders from the north, had established themselves as overlords long before the Spaniards under Cortez arrived in 1519—we shall find a somewhat similar state of affairs. What we shall find is most horrible, but it is well that we should be reminded that in the expression of their religious ideas, in their ideas of the gods and of the right form of worship, men have sometimes committed the most dreadful crimes and perpetrated the most awful atrocities. So it was in not so very ancient Mexico. From the carvings and manuscripts that have survived, and from the accounts given by the Catholic priests and others who were in Cortez' army, we have a picture of the religious festivals of the Aztecs that reminds one all too forcibly of " man's inhumanity to man."

One of the principal deities of the Aztecs was Chicomecohuatl, the Maize Goddess, whose great festival was celebrated annually in the autumn. On this occasion she was impersonated by a slave-girl of twelve or thirteen years of age, who was chosen for her beauty of face and figure. The priests invested her with the ornaments of the goddess, putting a mitre on her head, hanging necklaces of bright yellow maize-cobs round her neck, and fastening in her hair an upright green feather to represent the ear of maize. This they did, we are told, because the maize was not yet quite ripe, and so was very properly symbolized by a girl who was still

CHICOMECOHUATL
(*British Museum*)

of tender years, not yet a woman. For a day the priests led the poor little girl through the streets, showing her proudly at every house in turn, and allowing her to play in her strange finery, while she was unconscious of her approaching doom.

In the evening all the people gathered in the temple, and spent the night listening to the solemn music of trumpets, flutes, and horns, by the light of

129

a multitude of lamps and candles. Then at midnight a kind of portable chair was brought in, and in it was placed the girl, now half stupefied with the excitement and lack of sleep.

Around her the grim-faced priests swing their censers, filling the air with intoxicating odours. The music strikes up, and then suddenly the head priest whips out his knife and snips off the green feather and the lock of hair to which it is attached. These he presents to the image of the great Maize Goddess that stands, covered with maize-cobs and greenery, in the shadows at the back of the temple. As he does so, he weeps and prays, and all the people weep and pray with him, in the hope and in the belief that the goddess will listen to them and send a bumper harvest. The supplications being ended, the little girl is allowed to descend from her chair, and is taken away to spend the rest of the night in peace—her last night on earth.

While she sleeps, or tries to sleep, the crowds remain awake in the warm night, moving slowly about the temple courts.

Morning comes, and again the priests produce the girl who is to be the victim, dressed as before in her mitre and necklace of maize-cobs, and the costume of the goddess. Again she mounts the chair, and she is carried to the image of the goddess whom she is supposed to impersonate. She is allowed to get out again, and as before the image she stands, ankle-deep in the offerings of corn and fruits that strew the floor, she is approached by all the elders and the nobles of the city, and then by the most respected and highly placed matrons. Each holds a little saucer, which contains dried blood that they have drawn from their ears by way of penance during the past seven days of fasting. The dried blood they scrape off and cast down before the girl, intending it as an offering to the Maize Goddess.

Now there is a " break " while the people go home and feast just as good Christians (says the old Spanish chronicler who describes the scene) partake of meat and other food at Easter, after the long weeks of Lenten abstinence. After which they return to the Temple to see the last scene.

It is not long now. The girl—let us hope she is drugged into complete stupor—is solemnly incensed by the priests. Then she is suddenly flung on her back on a heap of corn and her head is struck off. The priests splash her blood on the wooden image of the goddess, the walls, the offerings piled up on the floor. A still more horrible thing is to come. The corpse is flayed, and one of the priests dresses himself in the girl's skin, dons the robes she had worn, and is taken in procession through the streets.

Why They Killed the Goddess

An awful rite, and it may well have shocked the Spaniards who saw it, accustomed though they were to the grim scenes of the battlefield, not to mention the fires lit around heretics condemned by the Inquisition.

Why was there so horrible a practice? The answer suggested is that the girl victim received the thanks and the homage of the people because she was for the time being the Maize Goddess. Being but a girl, she represented very fittingly the young corn. She was killed in order that her blood should invigorate the growing crop. And finally, the horrid rite at the last, when the priest capered about in her clothes and skin, was intended to ensure that the death of the goddess should be followed immediately by her resurrection.

In many parts of the world similar ritual murders have been practised as part of the religious procedure, and, as Frazer says, we may infer with some degree of probability that the practice of killing a human representative of a deity has commonly been regarded simply as a way of perpetuating the divine energies in the fullness of youthful vigour, untainted by the weakness and frailty of age, from which they must have suffered if the deity had been allowed to die a natural death.

SEPTEMBER

VERY different from the grim and grisly scene we have just witnessed are the sights and sounds of the traditional harvest-home in the British countryside. Since the invention of machinery much of the old-world charm has departed : there is not much poetry in the swift efficiency of the combine-harvester as it cuts the corn in great swathes, sweeps up the stalks and binds them in neat bundles, and then flings them aside to be picked up later. But here and there, and particularly, of course, in the more out-of-the-way parts and in the more hilly and rugged districts, human sweat and toil are the main instruments in harvesting, as they have been from time immemorial. The Bible has many a reference to harvests and harvesting—you remember the lovely story of Ruth, gleaning in the barley-fields of Boaz ?—and English literature is rich in harvest sounds and scenes.

Here, for instance, is Robert Chambers, a writer of the middle years of the last century, who waxes eloquent in his description of the graceful way in which the good reaper handles his sickle and clutches the corn—one sweep (he says) and the whole armful is down, and laid so neat and level, that when the band is put round the sheaf every straw touches the ground when the sheaf is stood up. Then he talks of the rich morsels of colour about the cornfield when the reapers are at work. The handkerchiefs which they bind round their foreheads to keep off the sun—the white of the rolled-up shirt-sleeves—the gleaners' dresses of every hue, blue, red, and grey, as they stoop or stand here and there, while over all is the great blue expanse of heaven, with just a few white clouds drifting lazily along. In such a light the white horses seem cut out of silver and the chestnuts of ruddy gold, while the black ones stand out against the sky as if carved in marble.

Pretty, indeed, must have been the sight of the young children gleaning, each with a little bag or pocket and a pair of scissors to cut off the straw. Rare gleaning was it in those days, when the kindly farmers allowed the poor—widows with little children in particular—to pick up what ears they could, to make into bread against the coming winter.

Queen of the Harvest

Then our writer goes on to describe the high-piled waggon—the Hock Cart it was called—rocking over the furrowed fields and sweeping through the narrow lanes as the last of the harvest was carried home. All the village turned out to see the final load driven into the rick-yard—the toothless old grandmother, squinting through her spectacles as she stood at her cottage door, and the poor old labourer, now sick and ailing so that he will never again " give a hand," leaning on his stick and thinking of the days when he was a mighty man with the scythe and pitchfork. One sheaf—here is a relic of old pagan custom and belief, for it may have represented the old Roman goddess Ceres—the last sheaf in the field, was often decorated with flowers and ribbons; this is the sheaf that in certain parts of England and Scotland used to be called the " Kern Doll." Sometimes a pretty girl sat on top

A KERN DOLL

of the load or astride one of the great fat horses, her straw hat ornamented with blue cornflowers and yellow ears of corn. Right proud was she to be chosen by the harvesters as the " Maiden " or the " Queen of the Harvest." As one old poet says:

> Home came the jovial Hockey load,
> Last of the whole year's crop,
> And Grace among the green boughs rode,
> Right plump upon the top.

Right proud was the driver as he flicked his whip on coming through the gate; and right proud, too, was the farmer as he stood with his wife and daughter beside him, to see the last load safely home.

Best of all was the harvest supper in the great barn, when the farmer made merry with the men and women who had helped him in his labours. As the seventeenth-century poet Robert Herrick puts it,

> You shall see first the large and cheefe
> Foundation of your Feast, Fat Beefe;
> With Upper Stories, Mutton, Veale
> And Bacon, (which makes full the meale)
> With sev'rall dishes standing by,
> As here a Custard, there a Pie,
> And here all tempting Frumentie . . .

There's that which drowns all care, stout Beere;
Which freely drink to your Lord's health,
Then to the Plough, the Commonwealthe . . .
Then to the Maids with Wheaten Hats:
To the rough Sickle, and crookt Sythe,
Drink frollick boyes, till all be blythe.
Feed, and grow fat. . . .

Altogether it was a jovial business, a delightful break in the daily round of toil—a time of rejoicing and of deep thankfulness to the God of the harvest who had provided good and abundant food for yet another year.

The Harvest of the Vines

What the corn harvest is to the peoples of northern Europe, the grape harvest—the *vendange*—is to those who live in the more genial climates of the south. If during the last week in September or the first week or two in October we were to visit the Rhineland and Alsace, the Champagne country of France, the Apennine slopes in Italy, the terraces beside the Lake of Geneva, and the country that lies about Bordeaux and the estuary of the Gironde, we should find the shops shut and nearly everyone gone away. But they would not be gone very far; only to the vineyards on the nearby hills, where they might be found—townsfolk working beside the peasants—stripping the vines of their heavy bunches of purple or white grapes.

It is a fascinating sight to watch, as the scissors go snip! snip! in the blazing sunshine, and bunch after bunch drops with a soft thud into the basket. When the basket is full, a young man comes up carrying a metal container, into which he tips the load of grapes. When his container is full in its turn, he pours out the grapes into a big wooden cask placed in a wagon. The grapes are packed into this as tightly as they will go, and before long a thin purple stream begins to overflow. Then the wagon moves off, dragged by its heavy cart-horse, to where stand the winepress and the wine-vats.

Meanwhile the picking goes on in the vineyards. Some of the workers—men, women, girls, and boys—are more expert than others, and when they reach the end of their rows they wait for the others to catch up. Then, when all are ready, they move on together to attack another section of the field. For nine hours or so they labour, every day of the week, including Sunday (but they are expected to attend early morning Mass first), and before the harvest is over the normally white-faced clerks and shop-assistants are burnt and bronzed as if they had worked in the fields from childhood.

Great care is taken to see that no stalks or leaves are pressed with the grapes. The actual pressing is done by machinery, and the juice is pumped into the vats, where it ferments for three weeks or so. Then it is piped into huge casks, and remains there for a matter of three years. After which it will be bottled and labelled, sold to the wholesalers, and so start on its journey to the table in some distant restaurant or home.

This is the procedure in the Bordeaux country, and in other districts where the wine is made as a commercial proposition. Where the vine is grown merely to produce the local drink, the methods will be much more crude. Thus in the rural districts of Italy one may see peasants with bare feet jumping up and down on a squelching mass of grapes in a cart, while the juice runs out at the back into a cask placed in the dusty road beneath. It is not to be wondered at that such wine is rougher to the taste than that produced for export.

When all the vines have been cut, there is the harvest-home, when the peasants delight to put on their traditional costumes, engage in some kind of procession or festival, and sit down to supper together. It is pleasant indeed to see the beautifully-decorated wagons being dragged through the streets by fat horses or lumbering oxen, and to watch the girls in their gaily striped skirts and tightly-laced bodices, their black curls kept in order by brightly-coloured handkerchiefs, holding on to the vast cask as the wagon rumbles and rolls over the cobbles. The maidens fling their tambourines, the children cheer, and the old people smile as, standing in the sun, their thoughts go back to the vintage celebrations of long, long ago, when they and the world were young together.

So it has been for thousands of years, for man must have discovered that the vine produced something that was good to drink not long after he found the way of putting seed into the ground and making out of it in due course a cake or a loaf.

Learning from Osiris

The ancient Egyptians said that Osiris, the great god, once reigned as a king on earth ; it was he who reclaimed the Egyptians from savagery, gave them good laws, and taught them to eat corn—before his

time they had been cannibals, eating one another—
and how to squeeze out the grape-juice and turn it
into wine.   After which, leaving Egypt in the care of
the goddess Isis, who was his sister and also his
queen, Osiris set out on a missionary journey to convert other people to a diet of corn and wine.   In
some countries the vine would not grow, and so there
he taught the inhabitants how to make a very good
drink by brewing beer from barley.   But whenever
possible he taught the benefits of vine-cultivation,
and when he returned to Egypt he was rich with the
presents that the grateful people had showered
upon him.

In ancient Greece they used to worship a god of
the vine—Bacchus, or Dionysus, he was named—
and at various times of the year, coinciding with
important stages in the vine cultivation, the peasants
celebrated in dance and song and feast.

The Strange Story of Dionysus

Dionysus, according to the old Greek myth, was
the son of Zeus, the King of the Gods, and the
Princess Semele, the daughter of the King of Thebes.
Semele seems to have been a very silly young
woman, for she prayed that Zeus should visit her
in all his divine splendour ; he did so, and the poor
girl was burnt up by his lightning.   But Zeus
rescued her baby and placed him in his thigh,
whence in due time he was born.   He was a highly
precocious child, and the nymphs of Nisa, who were
entrusted with his unbringing, must have found him
a " handful."   When he grew up he was often
persecuted by those who refused to credit his

divine parentage, and these he rendered mad by way of showing that he really was the son of Zeus. But those who believed his story he blessed abundantly. In particular, he showed them the art of cultivating the vine, and it is hardly surprising that those who were shown the method soon took advantage of it to their own hurt. Like so many others since, they " didn't know when to stop," and sober drinking

DANCING MAENADS (*from an ancient Greek cup*)

developed into tippling, and tippling into downright drunkenness.

So it came about that the beautiful young god was accompanied on his wanderings by crowds of votaries, both men and women, who danced and sang and generally displayed their high spirits in an abandoned fashion. The men were known as satyrs and the women as maenads—the word means " mad women "—and Bacchantes (from Dionysus's alternative name). They danced around him in half-mad ecstasy, and sometimes they captured and killed bulls and other animals and gorged themselves on the raw and reeking flesh.

Another form of the Dionysus myth says that he was the son of Zeus and Persephone, and that hardly had he been born when he mounted his father's throne and mimicked him by brandishing the lightning in his baby hand. But he did not enjoy his greatness long. Hera, Zeus's lawful wife, was intensely jealous, and sought a way to destroy her rival's child. One day she bribed the guards whom Zeus (or Jupiter, as the Romans called him) had put on the nursery door, entered the room, and amused the child with rattles and a magic looking-glass and suchlike toys until the horrid Titans, whom she had engaged for the purpose and who were her devoted servants, rushed in and slew him. They cut up his body into small pieces, boiled them, and then ate them, since they were cannibals.

When Zeus heard of the crime, he was furious. With a great stroke of his lightning he burnt up the Titans. From their ashes (we are told) sprang the races of men, and that is why men have such mixed natures—the divine aspect comes from Zeus, by way of the flesh of Dionysus that the Titans had devoured, while the savage and bestial aspect is derived from the Titans themselves.

Very likely the story of Dionysus was not just a myth, but a legend—that is, it was not entirely fanciful. There may have been some enterprising fellow who thought out and discovered the arts of the vine and wine, and who came to a sad and bad end in some drunken revel. Certain it is that in various parts of the Greek-speaking world the story of Dionysus was represented in every detail. His worshippers danced in the woodland glades to the music of flutes and cymbals, to indicate the toys with which he had been lured to his doom, and then they attacked live bulls and tore them with their teeth. In some strange way Dionysus came to appear as a suffering god, who was killed and buried and came to life again, and it is supposed that he was the symbol of the death of vegetation in Winter and its revival in Spring. So in yet another form we encounter this old, old myth. In the Dionysian worship there were " Mysteries," just as there were at Eleusis in connection with the worship of Demeter and Persephone. As likely as not there were representations of the god's birth and death and joyful resurrection. The story was widely believed, and as late as the first century of our era we find Plutarch (the Greek author of the famous *Lives*) consoling his wife on the death of their baby daughter with the tale that was told in the Dionysian mysteries. The young god died and rose again from the dead : in somewhat similar fashion, the soul of the infant girl, the souls of her loving father and mother, will survive the fact of death. . . .

A Fat Goose at Michaelmas

Returning now to England, we arrive on September 29—Michaelmas Day, or, as it is described in the Church calendar, the day of St. Michael and All Angels. St. Michael is regarded by Christians as one of the chief angels, an archangel, and he is described in the Bible as one who is the captain of the angelic hosts against the Devil and his agents. In the stained-glass windows of churches one may often see him pictured as an armour-clad knight, trampling on the fallen Lucifer or Satan. The Mohammedans, too, hold him in high regard as one of the four chief angels. Why he should be connected with September 29 is not at all clear. Much more obvious is the reason for the day's association with geese. For centuries up to not so long ago it was the custom at Michaelmas (St. Michael's Mass) for tenants to bring a goose as a present to their landlord when paying their rent—with a view, we may suppose, to making him the more willing to overlook any small deficiency in the sum due, or to persuade him not to turn them out in favour of another tenant. At this time of the year the bird was found to be at its best for eating, since it had grown fat on the stubble left after the corn had been cut. So the belief grew up that if one had " a fat goose on St. Michael for dinner," as an eighteenth century writer puts it, " then all the year round I shall not want for money."

' Nuts and Tricks ' with the Primroses

Michaelmas Eve was a period of merry-making in the England of our ancestors. Thus we read in *The Vicar of Wakefield* that Parson Primrose, his wife, and children were invited " to burn nuts and play tricks at neighbour Flamborough's " on that day. One of the games was blind-man's buff, and, Goldsmith makes Mr. Primrose say, " my wife too was persuaded to join in the diversion, and it gave me pleasure to think she was not yet too old."

There followed " hot cockles " (a game in which one of the players was blindfolded, and, being struck, had to guess who had hit him); then " questions and commands "; and finally they all sat down to hunt the slipper.

As every person may not be acquainted with this primeval pastime [says the good old parson], it may be necessary to observe, that the company in this play plant themselves in a ring upon the ground, all except one, who stands in the middle, whose business it is to catch a shoe, which the company shove about under their hams from one to another, something like a weaver's shuttle. As it is impossible, in this case, for the lady who is up to face all the company at once, the great beauty of the play lies in hitting her a thump with the heel of the shoe on that side least capable of making defence. It was in this manner that my eldest daughter [Olivia] was hemmed in, and thumped about, all blowzed, in spirits, and bawling for fair play, with a voice that might deafen a ballad-singer. . . .

OCTOBER

THE Mohammedan calendar is not the same as ours. Not only does it start from the year of the Hegira, the " flight " of the Prophet Mohammed from Mecca to Medina in A.D. 622, but it is lunar, and the year is some eleven days shorter than our year. The Mohammedan months do not always fall at the same seasons of the year. Sometimes a festival will occur in the hot season, shall we say; gradually, as the years pass, it will fall a little earlier, until it may be in the equivalent of winter. This is sometimes very inconvenient, as when the great fast of Ramadan falls in the most trying period of the year.

Our calendar is not lunar but solar, that is, it is related to the annual movements of the Sun and not to the monthly movements of the moon. So it is that Christmas always falls at the same time every year, and is always in the winter. The same is true of a number of other festivals, but (as we have seen) it is not true of Easter, which is not " fixed " but is a movable feast.

All this is by way of introduction to the fact that it is not possible to say that the great festivals and fasts of Mohammedanism or Islam fall on a certain day in June or December, or any other month. The equivalent day varies from year to year.

Hegira year 1369 began on October 24, 1949. That is why we may very properly concern ourselves in this " October " chapter with the great festival or celebration of Moharram. This is the name of the first month of the Mohammedan or Moslem year, and in most parts of the Moslem world it is the occasion for a kind of religious drama, recalling one of the saddest and best-remembered episodes in the history of Mohammedanism.

The Prophet Mohammed died at Medina in A.D. 632, and he was followed in the Caliphate, i.e. in the supreme leadership of the Mohammedan church and nation, by three of his " Companions " in turn—Abu Bekr, Omar, and Othman. Mohammed had left no son, but his only daughter, Fatima, was married to his cousin Ali, and many Moslems thought that Ali ought to become Caliph. Eventually he did so, in A.D. 655, when Othman had been assassinated. But after five years Ali too fell a victim to an assassin's dagger; whereupon Moawiya, his chief rival, refused to acknowledge Ali's elder son Hasan as Caliph and assumed the title himself. After some years Hasan was poisoned —at least, so some historians say; and his claim to the Caliphate passed to his brother Hussein. Moawiya was dead by now, and the war that broke out was between his son Yezid, and Hussein, Mohammed's grandson.

Hussein's Tragic Fate

There was not much of a fight. Hussein was trapped on the plain of Kerbela in Iraq, with but a hundred and fifty men to oppose a force of three thousand sent by Yezid. One by one the little band were killed or wounded, and at last only Hussein and his son were left. Hussein sat on the ground, and the little boy ran about him, while all around lay the dead and dying. None of the enemy was anxious to kill the Prophet's grandson. Then a chance arrow struck the little boy and he fell dead. Hussein laid the corpse gently on the ground. " We come from Allah, and we return to Allah," he murmured. He stooped down to drink some water from the Euphrates which flowed close by, and as he did so an arrow struck him in the mouth. The spell was broken. His enemies rushed up, and pierced him through and through with their swords and spears.

So began the great division of the Moslem world that has endured to the present time. One great party—the larger, in fact—called the Sunnis, do not hold Ali in special regard ; but the other, known as the Shiahs, remember Hussein as a martyr, and around his head cluster all the ideas of self-sacrifice, submission to the Will of Allah (God), and uncomplaining bravery in the face of disaster, that have made a particularly strong appeal to the Persian mind. Another reason why the Persians venerate Hussein so deeply is that he was engaged to be married to the daughter of the Persian king.

This, then, is the story that is the subject of the great " Passion Play " performed every year in Persia and other parts of the Moslem world where the Shiahs are numerous. (Perhaps it should be said that " Passion " here has no connection with bad temper : it comes from the Latin for " suffering," and means just that.)

On the first day of Moharram begins a period of

increasing mourning, and for ten days no marriages are celebrated, no new things are bought, no new house is begun ; woman are careful not to put on a new dress, and do not use the slightest " make-up " ; in the streets there is no laughter, voices are subdued, and many social functions are " taboo." At service-time towards evening the mosques are packed with Moslems, who shed tears and mourn as

A *TAZIA* IN THE MOHARRAM PROCESSION

if the " Battle of Martyrs " was fought quite recently, instead of nearly thirteen centuries ago. The walls are draped with black cloth, and there is erected a temporary structure—a *tazia*—supposed to represent Hussein's tomb or mausoleum. A band of singers is employed to chant the fallen hero's praises. After about an hour of the monotonous music the " Reciter of Events " mounts the pulpit, seats himself on the upper step, and proceeds to relate in dramatic form the incidents of the battle. " It is a strange story," he begins, " a cruel fate that befell the bone and blood of the Prophet himself." " Aye, aye ! " respond the audience, with deep groans. " It is time for you to listen and to shed tears," goes on the Reciter, " tears of blood about the tragedy of Hussein." Then he acts the slaying of Hussein's little boy, and the death of Hussein himself. The hearers are gradually worked up to a terrific pitch of emotion. Some fall down exhausted. Some beat their breasts in the most savage fashion, and tear their clothes. Some faint and drop to the ground with the excitement. Men's groans and women's wails form a medley of mourning.

On the tenth day, the Day of Ashrah it is styled, there is a procession. The miniature mausoleums are taken round the streets, and every hundred yards or so a stop is made to recite verses, or to act a scene from the battle, or to indulge in a fresh out-burst of deepest mourning. Here and there sherbet or water is handed out free to everyone who asks, as a reminder of the fact that the followers of Hussein were refused permission by their foes to slake their thirst. At about noon all the *tazias* meet in the main square ; and soon after another procession appears, this time of men impersonating the soldiers who fought for Hussein, a hundred horses, a number of camel-riders, a horse supposed to represent Hussein's steed, and seven heads— they are really lemons—carried on lances, just as Yezid's men bore the heads of Hussein and his fellow-martyrs. The Passion Play now arrives at its climax. The vast crowd lift their arms as one man, and then bring down their fists "thud ! " on their bare chests. " What happened to Hussein ? " they roar or wail. " What happened to Hussein ? " And the answer comes, " Hussein was made a martyr." Again and again the uplifted arms, the clenched fists, the volley of thuds ; again and again is made the clamorous reminder of " what happened to Hussein."

It is said that fatal accidents are by no means uncommon in the Moharram celebration, and that the hospitals are busy for weeks with cases of exposure and wounds and mental distress.

Oberammergau's Sacred Drama

To Christians " Passion Play " means a religious drama in which the Passion of Jesus Christ is represented. The most famous—although it is not the only one—is that given at the little Bavarian village of Oberammergau ; this was first performed in 1633, when the plague was devastating Germany, and the villagers vowed that if the pestilence passed them by, they would produce the Passion Play every ten years by way of acknowledgment of the Divine mercy. The performance has been given every ten years since 1680, with the exception of the periods of the two World Wars. In modern times huge audiences have been attracted, drawn more particularly by the fine, deeply sympathetic, and reverent acting of Josef Mayr and then Anton Lang, who have taken the part of Christ. Usually sixty or seventy performances are given in the summer months. All the players are villagers, and to be chosen for a part is regarded as a very high honour.

The Passion Play begins at 8 a.m. and lasts until

late afternoon. The chief incidents are Christ's triumphal entry into Jerusalem, Judas arranging his Master's betrayal with the Chief Priests, the Last Supper in the upper room at Jerusalem, the betrayal and arrest in the garden of Gethsemane, Judas' suicide, the trial and condemnation of Jesus before Pilate, the agonizing procession to Calvary and the crucifixion, the descent from the cross, and the entombment in the garden. The play ends on the victorious note of the women coming very early in the morning, and finding that Christ has risen.

The Hindus, too, have their Passion Plays, just as have Moslems and Christians. The most popular is the *Ram Lilla*, which is based on the story of Rama and his devoted wife Sita, given in the great epic poem known as the *Ramayana*.

The Undying Story of Rama and Sita

Rama was a young prince who lived in the India of long ago, perhaps centuries before the beginning of the Christian era. So noble was he, that Hindus believe that he was an incarnaton or *avatar* of Vishnu. The great poem opens with the story of Rama's wooing of Sita, as lovely and charming a princess as he was a handsome and gallant prince. But the King, Rama's father, has taken a new Queen, and at her request Rama is banished from the court in order that her own son should receive the royal inheritance. Very, very sadly and reluctantly the King agrees, and Rama is condemned to leave the luxurious palace to live for fourteen years in the pathless and houseless jungle.

Sita refuses to be separated from her husband

and demands that she shall be allowed to share his exile. She declares, as Romesh Chunder Dutt puts it in his translation of the epic,

For the faithful woman follows where her wedded lord may lead,
In the banishment of Rama, Sita's exile is decreed . . .
Sita steps before her husband wild and thorny paths to clear!

For my mother often taught me and my father often spake,
That her home the wedded woman doth beside her husband make,
As the shadow to the substance, to her lord is faithful wife,
And she parts not from her consort till she parts from fleeting life!

So the devoted pair go out into the jungle to share its perils together. For fourteen years their exile continues, and at home when the King dies, Rama's younger brother rules in his name, until he shall return; he refuses to seat himself on the throne, but places on it Rama's shoes as the symbol of his right.

The Passion Play goes on to tell of the way in which Sita is entrapped and stolen away by Ravana, the " Bad King " of Ceylon; how Rama, powerfully assisted by Hanuman, the Monkey-god, raises an army and goes to her rescue; how at length Ceylon is invaded, Ravana is killed by Rama, and Sita is brought back in triumph. So the Prince and Princess are reunited and live happily after.

Such in brief is the story of the *Ramayana*, a story which appeals as perhaps no other to the millions of India. Rama is the Hindu ideal of all that a man should be—brave, uncomplaining, trained to endure and to suffer, righteous through and through; while as for Sita, she (as Romesh Dutt says) holds a place in the hearts of Indian women which no other creation of a poet's imagination holds among any other nation on earth. " There is not a Hindu woman whose earliest and tenderest recollections do not cling round the story of Sita's sufferings and Sita's faithfulness, told in the nursery, taught in the family circle, remembered and cherished through life."

In the great Indian cities the scenes of the story are enacted in the open air in the autumn, as part of the celebrations of the Durga-puja, the festival held in honour of the wife of the god Siva. Youths dress up to represent Rama and Sita, and march in procession through the streets, preceded by drummers and trumpeters. Husband and wife are shown taking leave of their sorrowing friends in the palace, and disappearing into a forest grove; the great battles with Ravana are realistically reproduced, and some of the players wear " monkey faces " to represent the legions of Hanuman who helped Rama to win the day; Sita is seen walking barefoot over the embers of a fire, to prove to Rama beyond a doubt that the suspicions that in spite of himself he had harboured—that she had fallen a victim to Ravana's wiles during her captivity—were entirely without foundation. Finally, while conch horns are blown mightily and the drums throb and throb, an enormous effigy of Ravana, made of bamboo and paper and filled with fireworks, is erected; then Rama shoots a blazing arrow into its heart, and the " Demon King " goes up in flames amid the delighted shouts of the spectators. The ashes of the effigy are collected, and the simple folk take them home to be used as " cures " for eye trouble and other ills.

Dancers of the Wajang Wong

Not only in India but also in those islands of the East Indies where Hindu influence is strong, Passion Plays are enacted in which the great episodes of Indian mythology are represented in dramatic form. In Java, the *Wajang Wong* (as the national theatre is called) relies very largely on the themes of the *Ramayana* and the other great Indian epic, the

KRISHNA AND THE GARUDA-BIRDS

Mahabharata, of which the chief hero is the Hindu god Krishna. In both epics a prominent part is played by fabulous monsters, in particular the Garuda-birds, the Lords of the Air, who helped Rama to recover his stolen bride, and imparted to Krishna some of their wisdom. In the *Wajang Wong* the parts of those birds are played by young men garbed in costumes formed out of the feathers of several hundred hens, and there are other animal rôles

154

which require long and careful preparation. Some of the dances take an hour and a half to perform, so only men in a state of full physical fitness may undertake them. Only very seldom is a woman chosen for a female part. The costumes, the scenery, the production as a whole, present magnificent opportunities for the Javanese craftsmen to show their skill, and the result is usually an artistic masterpiece.

The Feast of Lamps

The last three days of the Indian year, falling in our October and twenty days after the Durga-puja, are taken up with the great Feast of Lamps (*Divali*, it is called), held in honour of Lakshmi, the goddess of wealth. The first day is considered to be exceedingly lucky. It is perhaps the best day in all the year on which to send a child to school for the first time, to move into a new house, to get married, and so on. There is a tremendous bustle of preparation, as before the feast begins everything must be as bright and clean as may be. The bills of all the tradesmen and the wages of the servants must be paid. Those people who have no trust in banks but keep their money under the bed, take it out on the first day of Divali, wash the coins in milk or water, and then put them away again in the box or jar. When all is spick and span, the women put on their best clothes, light every lamp and candle in the house, and generally rejoice that another harvest has been safely garnered, another year's debts paid in full. The next day is also one of gladness and merry-making, and visits are paid to friends and relations. But that night is one when every respectable person keeps indoors. For it is the night when the witches and evil spirits get loose and rush about on their wicked errands. Then you may see the horrid ghosts of those who have been murdered, or have died suddenly by accident in the year that has gone. Even the ghosts of those who have died peacefully in their beds may be encountered. Some devout people hope to keep the ghosts away by putting little heaps of cakes at the cross-roads where the spectres are bound to see them. Others are more venturesome and draw circles in the dust of the road or in the cemetery, inside which they sit down and bid defiance to the wicked goblins by repeating over and over again sacred *mantras* or spells. But the last day of Divali is the happiest. The children, who have had a pretty good time so far, letting off crackers and generally enjoying themselves with hardly a reproof from their half-deafened elders, now light a lamp, place it in a lump of cow-dung, and take it round from house to house, very much as the children do in Scotland on New Year's Day. But they beg not for pennies but for oil for their lamp, and the reason they advance for appealing to your generosity is that the ancestors, wherever they may be, shall have light.

That afternoon is called the " Worship of the Account-Books," when all old accounts must be closed and new ones opened, and the lamps and other lights are larger and brighter than ever.

Worshipping the Account-Books

The Jains, too, celebrate Divali, in spite of the fact that their religion is opposed to that of the great mass of the Hindus. They say that it originated when Mahavira, the last of their great saints or *jinas*, passed into *moksha* (or, as we should say, died). Those who were present at the time declared that " Since the light of intelligence had gone out let us make an illumination of material matter." The first two days are observed in the same way as by the Hindus. It is on the third day that the Jains are said to worship their account-books, and in every corner of home and office they place a lighted lamp or candle. In the morning the more devout among them go to the nearest temple or monastery, where they listen to the chief monk as he tells them about the virtuous life of the great Mahavira and sing a hymn or two, after which they go home and make up their account-books for the past year. If everything is balanced and in order, the book is placed on a stool, and the high-caste Brahman who is the family chaplain paints a lucky mark on the forehead of the householder, on his pen, and on one page of his accounts. He then writes *Sri*—one of the names of Lakshmi— five, seven, or nine times on the account-book so as to make a pyramidal pattern. Next a rupee is placed between the pages of the book. This is supposed to represent Lakshmi, and it must be carefully kept all through the coming year. To lose it would be accounted most unfortunate. As often as not, the same coin is used year after year, so that in some Jain families it is quite a collector's piece. Then a creeper leaf is put between the pages, and the book is sprinkled with a red powder, and rice, nuts, and fruit are placed upon it. Finally the Jain and the Brahman gorge themselves with the sweetmeats.

The fourth day is New Year's Day; and the Jains, like their Hindu neighbours, visit their friends, and send cards to those who are away.

Travellers say that to see Divali at its best one should go to Benares, where at nightfall millions of little earthen lamps, fed with oil, are placed close together so that mansions and palaces, temples and minarets and domes, are outlined in fire. All the boats on the river are lighted, too; and viewed from the river the city makes a magnificent spectacle, one of fairylike splendour that cannot be matched in any other city of the world.

The ' Dusts ' of Grandmother Miki

Towards the end of October is held the Grand Autumn Festival of perhaps the most interesting of the sects or churches to which the Japanese may belong, in addition to the church—State Shinto—which is the national or official church of the whole people. This particular sect is called Tenri Kyo—that means, " Teaching of the Divine Reason "—and it is a religion which is very much like the Christian Science that we have in this country and in America.

Just as the founder of Christian Science was a woman—Mrs. Mary Baker Eddy—so the founder of Tenri Kyo was a woman, who lived at much the same time. Her name was Omiki San, or Miki for short, and she was born and brought up in a little village, near where her parents had a farm, in Honshu. She went to the village school, where she was particularly good at needlework, and in 1810, when only twelve, was married to a young farmer of twenty-three.

She had six children, and was a first-rate mother. When she was about forty her life became altogether changed, following a religious experience. She went into a trance for hours; and when she came to, she announced that she was now the house, as it were, of a divine personage called the Commander of Heaven. It is this event that is remembered each year on October 26. Always she had been a very good woman, kind to everyone, and ready to take no end of trouble in helping the poor and ill. Now she insisted on giving to the poor and needy all that she possessed. Her husband and the children were not at all pleased when she sold the furniture and gave away the proceeds. Every time they refurnished, she did the same thing, so that when her husband died she was left practically penniless. Her relations and friends would have no more to do with her; her neighbours said she was bewitched, and was possessed by the spirit of a fox or a badger. Sometimes they set the police on her track, and she was whipped and put in prison for teaching doctrines that were not those that were officially approved. Altogether she had a very bad time of it, and she was so poor that often she had to sit sewing and spinning far into the night in order to earn a little money to keep herself and her two youngest children from starving.

After many years of this unhappy life, people began to take pity on her, and to be more friendly. Some believed that what she said was the truth, and joined the church that she had started. And what was her teaching? Well, it was just the sort of doctrine that one would expect from a good housewife. All the evils of life, she declared, are caused by dust—not ordinary dust, but eight special kinds, viz. too much hankering after food and drink, property, fame, wealth, and so on ; stinginess ; love that is not of the best kind, as when a mother spoils her " little darling " ; hatred and suspicion ; the spirit of revenge, malice, or spite ; anger ; pride and insolence ; and, finally, selfishness. All these " dusts " must be got rid of, said Mrs. Nakayama—that was her married name—by a kind of spring-cleaning. People must believe in goodness and truth, and then they will have no room in their hearts for the " dusts " which make them and other people miserable. She wrote a number of books, with such pleasant titles as *The Tip of the Writing-brush*, *Dancing Psalms*, and *The Ancient Chronicle of the Mud-sea*, and these form the " Bible " of the Tenri Kyo.

" Grandmother Miki " died in 1889, and not long ago it was stated that her followers numbered five millions. There are young men's and young women's societies connected with the movement, thousands of local churches, and a college for train-ing missionaries, who carry her gospel into all parts of Japan and even to countries overseas. Every day, at home or in church or wherever they may be, the members of this Japanese sect pray that the " Won-derful King of Divine Reason " will " sweep away evil "—the dusts, that is—" and save us."

Ancient History of Hallowe'en

Now we come to the last day of October, the 31st, which we know as Hallowe'en or All Hallow's Eve.

The word comes from the Anglo-Saxon *helig*, " holy," and the " eve " is the one before All Saints' or All-Hallows Day, November 1. But long before it was given a Christian complexion, as it were, the " eve " was a pagan festival, marking (as is clear from its old Gaelic name of Samhuinn in Scotland and Samhain in Ireland) the " summer-end." The ancient Celtic peoples of the British Isles thought that there were two suns—the " big sun of summer " and the " little sun of winter," and the latter " took over " at the time October turned into November, and continued its sway until about the beginning of May, when was observed the old heathen festival of Beltane.

These two dates, the end of April and the beginning of November, it has been pointed out, do not coincide with either the solstices or the equinoxes, nor with the principal seasons—sowing and reaping —of the agricultural year. But in Europe May 1 and November 1 are nevertheless turning-points, the one ushering in the warmer days and fresh vegetation, and the other giving warning of the near approach of winter. To the husbandman the dates are not important, but to the herdsman they are, since in May he leads out his flocks and herds to pasture on the young grass, while at the end of October he knows that the time has come to recall them from the open fields and house them in byre and fold. Thus there would seem to be good reason to believe that Hallowe'en and May-day are relics of the age before the invention of agriculture, when the Celts had not yet settled down to farming but were mainly a pastoral people, dependent on their herds for food and drink. There is evidence that in ancient Ireland the New Year used to begin on November 1.

Hallowe'en is one of the nights in the year which have been associated in particular with witches. The other is the eve of May-day—Walpurgis Night, as it is called after Walpurga, a Sussex-born damsel who in the eighth century accompanied her brother Willibrod and their uncle St. Boniface to Germany as Christian missionaries. She was so good a woman that she became a saint, and it is hard to discover any connection between her and the wicked old hags who were supposed to ride through the air on broomsticks and work evil on men and animals and plants. But it was decided that her " day " should be May 1, which had been for many, many centuries a heathen festival. On the evening before, the witches—as we may read in Goethe's *Faust*— were supposed to meet on the heights of the Brocken in central Germany, and there lay plans for the further ruin of mankind, for the blasting of man's harvests and herds and everything that is his. In course of time it came to be thought that St. Walpurga was powerful against such devilry.

Witches and Wizards on the War-path

Of all the superstitions that have made men miserable, the belief in witchcraft is one of the worst— perhaps *the* worst. For ages it was seriously and almost universally believed that there were beings —female witches, and wizards or male sorcerers— who had entered into a deliberate pact with Satan, the Devil, to do his bidding and work his will in return for material gain, for unholy pleasure, or just for the power of controlling the lives of others. The actual existence of a personal Devil or Evil One was most confidently believed in. Thousands of people professed to have seen him—sometimes in the shape of an animal, sometimes as a black man with horns and a tail, sometimes as a young and most lovely woman. It was a common belief that he visited people in their sleep, and any particularly ugly and mischievous child was said to be the "spawn of Satan." Under the chief Devil were believed to work a vast host of lesser devils or demons or evil spirits, whose chief activity was the plaguing of unhappy mortals and the leading of them into temptation and sin. (Our word "nightmare" is a relic of this ancient superstition, since *mara* is the Old High German word for an incubus, i.e. a male devil who was supposed to visit women in their sleep.) Educated and uneducated, priests and people alike, were absolutely convinced of the existence of a huge army of devils under the captaincy of Satan, and of men and women who were their allies for ill.

Witches and wizards were supposed to meet once a week in *esbats*, and to hold at regular intervals "sabbaths" at which they worshipped the Devil in person, danced and sang and feasted, made magic potions, devised spells, and practised many a wicked rite. Occasionally they were supposed to sacrifice a newborn child.

It has been the custom to smile at the belief in the witches and their sabbaths on Walpurgis Night and Hallowe'en. But up to even two hundred years ago witchcraft was no laughing matter. Tens of thousands of unhappy women have been executed—strangled or drowned or burnt alive—for asserting that they were in association with the Devil, or because they were accused of being his servants. Records have been preserved of many of the trials of alleged witches, from which it is plain that the learned judges had never a doubt on the subject. The accused often confessed to the charges laid against them. Of all the victims, perhaps the greatest and noblest was Joan of Arc, who was burnt alive in the market-place of Rouen as a witch in 1431.

Sometimes the charges were very serious, amounting to murder by poison and such like ; sometimes, however, the indictment was almost childish. Thus in 1665, in Charles II's reign, two Suffolk women were accused at Bury St. Edmunds of bewitching a number of their neighbours, and it was alleged that they had caused a girl to cough up a number of pins, a cart to be overturned twice or thrice in the same day and to be stuck between the gate-posts, pigs to die suddenly, and one poor man to be afflicted with lameness and to be so " vexed with a great number of lice of an extraordinary bigness, that although he many times shifted himself, yet he was not anything the better, but would swarm again with them ; so that in the conclusion he was forced to burn all his clothes, being two suits of apparel, and then was clean of them." Such were the charges brought against Rose Cullender and Amy Duny ; and for these things " they were executed on Monday the 17th March following, but they confessed nothing."

The last conviction for witchcraft in England was

at Hertford in 1712, but the sentence was remitted. It was not until 1736 that it was enacted that no more prosecutions for witchcraft should take place. The last to perish in Europe as a witch is said to have been a servant-girl in Switzerland in 1782; she was the last of, so it has been estimated, 300,000 women who died a fearful death because they were supposed to be in league with Satan.

Survivors of the ' Old Religion '

What are we to make of this extraordinary chapter in human history? Was it just an example of mass-delusion on a tremendous scale? Were the judges, the witnesses, the accused who confessed—were they all deceived? So many people believe, but there are others who take the view that witchcraft was a sur-vival of the old religion of paganism, which persisted in country places and among the peasantry long after it had died out or had been suppressed by the Christian Church in the towns. In their view, the Devil who appeared at the Sabbaths was undoubtedly a man, playing the part of what originally was not a devil but a god. The flying through the air on broomsticks may be explained when we remember that in the half-underground huts of our ancestors the hole in the roof was the chimney and also the door. The belief that witches could transform themselves into animals is one that may still be found in many parts of the world. Possibly, too, the per-formers in the Sabbath ritual wore animal skins. Such a dress was assumed by the " sorcerers " of prehistoric times, as seems to be indicated by a famous wall-painting discovered in a French cave, which shows a man disguised with stag horns, reindeer mask, and the legs and tail of other animals. No doubt, too, some of the evil deeds that were laid to the charge of the witches and sorcerers were true enough—although it is only fair to say that probably just as often the potions and other medicines prepared by the magicians were mere " country cures " such as are confidently recommended by some farmers' wives today.

So there may well have been strange doings on Walpurgis Night and Hallowe'en. The " old religion " that the Christian missionaries had done their best to suppress altogether, lived on in out-of-the-way places, and the gods of the ancient Greeks and Romans had their worshippers in our own land, up to only a century or so ago.

" A Calf's Heart studded with Pins . . ."

Nor is witchcraft altogether extinct. Occasionally we may read in the newspapers of gipsies being charged with getting money by false pretences, even with exercising " withcraft, sorcery, or enchantment." At the beginning of this century a calf's heart, thickly studded with pins, thorns, and twigs, was found in the chimney of a cottage in Dorsetshire ; beyond a doubt this was an instance of a form of witchcraft that is still widely practised in Eastern lands, as it was in ancient Egypt and even in prehistoric times—if you want to destroy an enemy you make an image of him, or something that is supposed to represent his heart, and stick it through with pins, maltreat it, or destroy it. Then just before Hallowe'en there is, we are told, quite a rush on the chemists' shops in the East End of London for the gum-resin called dragon's-blood, which has been used by women from time immemorial as a charm to attract a lover or retain the love of a fickle husband. All you have to do is to mix the dragon's-blood with quicksilver, sulphur, and saltpetre, and throw the mixture on a clear fire at midnight, repeating the while a certain incantation. For helping lovelorn maidens in some such fashion in days gone by many an ancient dame has been pricked all over to find the insensible spot that would prove beyond a doubt that she was a witch; ducked in the river, when if she *sank* she was innocent; whipped, tortured on the rack or with thumb-screws; or burnt alive at the stake.

Welcome, the Hungry Ghosts

Yes, Hallowe'en has many a weird and awful association. It was regarded as a time when supernatural influences were most likely to be abroad. It was the night when the spirits of the dead were supposed to walk. It was but natural to suppose that with the approach of winter " the poor shivering hungry ghosts," as Frazer calls them, should be driven from the bare fields and the leafless woodlands to the shelter of the cottage with its familiar fireside, where those they had loved and who still remembered them placed a table of good cheer for their refreshment. When the bleak winds began to whistle, the cows trooped back from the summer

167

pastures to be cared for and fed in the stalls ; " could the good-man and the good-wife deny to the spirits of their dead the welcome which they gave to the cows ? "

And not only the dead. If a vigil were kept in the church porch on Hallowe'en as on Midsummer Eve, one might see flitting along the shapes of those who were to die before another year was out. The fairies were let loose to wander, and the hob-goblins were up and around. Divination was believed to be most easy and effective on that night, and spirits might be " called up " at will.

But, as Dame Glendinning says in Sir Walter Scott's novel *The Monastery*, " I ken there is little luck in Hallowe'en sights. . . ." Pressed to tell the story, she relates how when she was a " hempie " (romp) of nineteen or twenty, she

had mair joes [young men] than ane, but favoured none o' them ; and sae, at Hallowe'en, Father Nicolas, the cellarer, was cracking his nuts and drinking his brown beer with us, and as blythe as might be, and they would have me try a cantrip [trick] to ken wha suld wed me ; and the monk said there was nae ill in it, and if there was, he would assoil [absolve] me for it.

So away she went into the barn to winnow three " wechts of naething," that is, to go through the action three times of exposing corn to the wind so that the chaff should blow away ; it was the old belief that at the third throw the figure of the girl's lover would appear.

Sair, sair my mind misgave me for fear of wrangdoing and wrang-suffering baith ; but I had aye a bauld spirit. I had not winnowed the last wecht clean out, and the moon was shining bright upon the floor, when in stalked the presence of my dear Simon Glendinning, that is now happy. I never saw him plainer in my life than I did that moment; he held up an arrow as he passed me, and I swarf'd awa' wi' fright. . . ."

When she came round, they tried to make out that the arrow was but Cupid's shaft: " gude man, he liked not it should be said that he was seen out o' the body!" But, the old lady went on, " Mark the end o' it, Tibb: we were married, and the grey-goose wing was the death o' him after a'!" " As it has been of ower mony brave men," said Tibb; " I wish there wasna sic a bird as a goose in the wide warld. . . ."

Merry Games with Nuts and Apples

Another great Scottish writer reminds us that Hallowe'en was not always a gloomy time; on the contrary, it has been attended by many a happy pastime, by feasting and merry making. In Robert Burns's poem we are taken to the fireside of the Scottish peasant, where the lads and lassies crack nuts and make a game of doing what Dame Glendinning did.

> The auld guid-wife's well-hoordet nits
> Are round an' round divided,
> An' mony lads an' lasses' fates
> Are there that night decided.

Two nuts were placed in the bars of the fire-grate by a wistful girl, one representing herself and the other the lover she particularly fancied. If the latter nut cracked or jumped, it was a sign that the lover would prove unfaithful; if it blazed or burned, he had an affection for her; if the two nuts burned together, then the girl would be married to the man she loved.

> Jean slips in twa, wi' tentie [attentive] e'e;
>   Wha 'twas, she wadna tell;
> But this is *Jock*, and this is *me*,
>   She says in to hersel;
> He bleez'd owre her, an' she owre him,
>   As they wad never mair part;
> Till fuff! he started up the lum [chimney]
>   And Jean had e'en a sair heart
>   To see't that night.

Still another kind of love-divination is referred to in a later verse.

> Wee Jenny to her graunie says,
>   " Will ye go wi' me, graunie?
> I'll eat the apple at the glass,
>   I got frae uncle Johnie."

But the grandame " fuff't her pipe " in great indignation.

> " Ye little skelpie-limmer's-face!
>   I daur you try sic sportin',
> As seek the foul thief [the Devil] ony place,
>   For him to spae your fortune:
> Nae doubt but ye may get a sight!
>   Great cause ye hae to fear it;
> For mony a ane has gotten a fright,
>   An' liv'd an' died deleeret,
>   On sic a night."

Apples as well as nuts used to be employed in these Hallowe'en practices, and it is said that in the old pagan mythology of the Celts they were considered to be the " fruits of long life "; Avalon, the heaven of our ancient forebears, was the " land of apples." The apple is also an old symbol of love: Eve gave Adam an apple in the Garden of Eden.

170

One of the chief sports of Hallowe'en was ducking for apples dropped in a tub of water. Little boys were, as might be expected, particularly skilful at retrieving them in their mouths without handling them, but sometimes the apples were dropped into the water by the lassies, who mentally named each one, and then the young fellows came into the room

DUCKING FOR APPLES ON HALLOWE'EN

and tried their luck at the sport. Happy and confident indeed was the girl whose apple was picked out by the man 'she had set her heart upon.

Many another quaint old custom is associated with the desire of a girl to know the man she will, or ought to, marry; in fact, there is hardly a district in England or Scotland or Wales, perhaps Ireland too, where such used not to be practised. Some are still practised. One more may be mentioned.

An English maid may place her shoes beside her
bed in the form of a T, and then as she gets into bed
she whispers :

> I cross my shoes in the shape of a T
> Hoping this night my true love to see,
> Not in the best or worst array,
> But in the clothes of every day.

No one knows how such customs arose, who invented them, or when or where. Their origins are
lost in the long ago, when the people of this land
were still pagan and believed that the gods or spirits
or other supernatural beings were very near, and
might be induced to help those who approached
them in the proper frame of mind and performed the
little rites of magic and divination in the proper way.

Then there are the Hallowe'en bonfires, for this
last night of October has been just as popular a
night for kindling a fire as Midsummer Eve, or
as Beltane, the Celtic festival in early May. In the
Highlands of Scotland children used to gather ferns
and bracken and anything suitable to make a fire,
place them on a heap outside each cottage, and then,
as darkness fell, put a light to them. The scene was
romantic in the extreme as the " Samhnagan fires "
blazed in the night. When the fire had died down,
the ashes were carefully collected and made into a
ring, inside which each member of the household
placed a stone. Next morning, he or she whose
stone was found to have been moved or damaged,
was certain not to live another twelve-month. So
they believed in Perthshire, and a very similar belief
has been reported from Wales.

And the reason for these Hallowe'en bonfires ?

Surely it is not unreasonable to suppose that they were originally intended to " feed " the sun, to keep him alive, as day by day he seemed to move farther away, to set sooner and lower in the sky. Such bonfires are not to be seen now, leaping from the hills in a great circle of flame. But we have our bonfires on Guy Fawkes's Night, only a few days later, on November 5. Children today burn the " guy," but a thousand, perhaps two or three thousand, years before Guy Fawkes tried to make a bonfire of the Houses of Parliament in 1605, the young people who were our ancestors piled up their heaps, fired them with a torch, and then danced around and sometimes through them, in the belief that they were doing something to help the poor old sun and prevent him from disappearing altogether and for all the time.

NOVEMBER

THE 1st of November is All-Hallows, or All Saints' Day—the day on which the Christian Church remembers those holy men and women who are not commemorated on special days of their own. The festival dates from November 1, 608, when the great pagan temple of the Pantheon—the name indicates that it was the temple of " all the gods "— in Rome was converted into a Christian church ; but there is no doubt that (as we saw in the last chapter) the heathen had a festival at this time. The day is also All Souls' Eve, when those who have died in the past year, or in years gone by, are particularly remembered. All Souls' Day—November 2—is in Roman Catholic lands a solemn festival on which Masses are said for the souls of the dead who (it is believed) are detained in the intermediate state of Purgatory until they shall be sufficiently purified to enter Heaven.

In the ancient pagan world it was the festival of the dead, when those who had passed from human sight, but not from human love, were sadly and reverently remembered. It is an altogether natural thing that the dead should be so held in loving remembrance ; and there are some anthropologists who, having observed how practically universal this " cult of the dead " is, both among ancient peoples and the primitive peoples still surviving in the present age, have concluded that in it we may find the beginnings of religion. For a very important part of religion, if not the most important part, is concerned with the spirit world, with the after-life and those who enjoy or endure it. In some countries, religion is very largely a matter of remembrance of dead-and-gone ancestors.

Among the Chinese, " ancestor-worship," as it is generally styled—although there is really nothing in it of the nature of worship of the ancestors as divine

" Ancestor-worship " in a Chinese House

—is the most generally held form of religious expression. It is not so universal as it was in the days when there was an Emperor in Peking, who made sacrifices on the Altar of Heaven at stated times each year in honour of the Imperial Fathers, and it is said that Chinese architects often neglect nowadays to include in their plans for new houses a little room to contain the sacred tablets bearing the names of departed ancestors, before which offerings might be made on their birthdays or other family occasions. Up to quite recently it was the proper thing for the " worship " to be performed in the presence of a younger member of the family, who (as it were) impersonated all those who were to be held in remembrance. Candles were burnt before the tablets, paper money was offered, incense wafted, and little gifts of food and drink placed handy for the spirits. These rites, it is explained, were not intended otherwise than as an expression of thankfulness to the ancestors without whom those men and women forming the family today could never have been born. The national celebrations at Peking were at certain seasons of the year, the most important being at the winter solstice.

Candles to Guide the Dead

It is a very general belief that on All Souls' Eve (even more so than the day before, on Hallowe'en) the dead return from wherever they may be— usually, it would appear, the place is not a particularly agreeable one—to the homes on earth where once they lived, and there partake of a meal in company with their still living children or other descendants. It is an appealing belief, and associated with it are many beautiful and moving customs. Thus in some places lighted candles are put in the windows to enable the returning souls to find their way in the dark, and to bring to them some measure of warmth and comfort. In some parts of Europe one may see the candles burning on the gravestones in the churchyard. In Brittany the church bells toll mournfully, and those who have loved and lost go to the graves of their dear ones, kneel there barefooted, and murmur prayers for the repose of their souls; at the same time, back at home the fire is kept burning brightly, the lamp is lit, a substantial supper is prepared, and the curtains are pulled back so as to bid the returning spirit welcome if it passes that way. In the Vosges mountains of France the peasants not only lay a meal but turn down the counterpane on the beds so as to convince the wandering spirits that there is still a place for them in their old home. Very similar customs are practised in Italy; and in Sicily little gifts of toys and sweets are laid by the parents on window-ledges and doorsteps, as the children have been taught to believe that when the ghosts come on All Souls' Day they never forget to bring with them some present for the children who, very likely, have been born since they went away.

Collecting for the ' Soul Cake '

There was formerly a custom in some districts of England and of Scotland to make on All Souls' Day a door-to-door collection of cakes and other food-stuffs, which were symbolically offered to the dead and then given to the poor. The collectors were young people of both sexes, and as they knocked at the door they said some such verse as this :

> Soul! Soul! for a soul cake!
> I pray, good mistress, a soul cake!
> An apple or a pear, a plum or a cherry,
> Any good thing to make us merry.
> One for Peter, two for Paul,
> Three for Him who made us all.
> Up with the kettle and down with the pan,
> Give us good alms and we'll be gone.

The Wicked Murder of Osiris

About the middle of November the ancient Egyptians had a festival of which one of the most important features was the illumination of the houses; it has been suggested that this was in the nature of an All Souls' celebration. Certainly this Egyptian festival was a solemn one, held in honour of the great and good god Osiris.

Osiris, it will be remembered, was a kind of Egyptian Bacchus or Dionysus. But he was very much more, as we shall see.

When he returned to Egypt after his travels, in which he had taught the nations the use of the vine and wine, Osiris was hailed by his people at home as a god. But his brother Set, a wicked fellow, was jealous of his renown and influence, and determined to destroy him. So he made a coffin-shaped box, just the right size to take Osiris, and induced the god-king—"just for a joke," as it were—to lie down in it. As soon as he had done so, Set slammed down the lid, fastened it up securely, and flung the box into the Nile.

When Isis, the wife and queen of Osiris—she was also his sister, as she was the sister of Set—heard the terrible news of the all-too-successful conspiracy, she mourned deeply and long, and sought here, there, and everywhere for her murdered lord's body.

For a long time she was unsuccessful. Nothing had been heard of the box with its precious contents. In fact, it had floated out into the Mediterranean and had been washed ashore on the coast of Syria, near the town of Byblus. There straightway a fine tree shot up and enclosed the box in its trunk. The king of the country admired the tree, and had it cut down and made into a pillar in his palace. But he did not discover what was hidden inside it.

In course of time Isis got word that the box had been washed ashore at Byblus ; and—to cut a long story short—she went to the royal palace, found the pillar, and implored the king to let her have it. Greatly wondering, the king granted her request, and Isis at once cut it open, and revealed the coffin in which Osiris' body lay. So she took it back to Egypt, and hid it while she went to see her son Horus. But unfortunately, Set happened to discover it in the moonlight, and this time he determined to make sure that his brother's corpse should be destroyed once and for all. He took it out of the box, cut it into little pieces, and flung them to the four winds.

When Isis returned, she was profoundly grieved at this fresh outrage, and she spent a long, long time searching for the pieces of Osiris's body. She found nearly all, and distributed them among a number of temples, whose priests gave them proper burial.

This is the story as told by the old Greek writers. But the Egyptians gave it a different ending. They said that when Isis and her sister Nephthys were lamenting over the corpse of Osiris, the Sun-God Ra took pity on them and sent the jackal-headed god Anubis down from heaven to be of some assistance. Anubis showed the sisters how to embalm Osiris, and then, when all was properly performed, Isis fanned the corpse with her wings, and thereupon

Osiris revived. Henceforth he ruled as sovereign of the Underworld. He was the Lord of Eternity, and the Egyptians came to believe that, just as he had

conquered and survived death, so they, too, might share in his glorious resurrection. Osiris lived again because he had been properly embalmed : if they were embalmed in the same thorough fashion, they would surely live on as he lived on in the world beyond the grave. So at the funerals of Egyptian believers in Osiris, the mourners made believe that the dead man *was* Osiris, and that they were Isis and Nephthys and those who had helped the divine sisters in their pious and holy task.

Later on, there were dramatic representations—" passion plays " —of the death of Osiris. An idol of the god, showing him as a king swathed in mummy-robes, was ceremonially buried, the while the priests smote their breasts, slashed their shoulders with knives, and wept and howled with grief. Then was enacted the search for the god-king's body, its retrieval, and

Osiris
THE GOD-KING

probably the method of restoring it to life. This was done at the November festival, and sculptures have been preserved showing the various scenes of the sacred drama—the dead king lying on his bier, and gradually raising himself, first to a sitting posture, then to a standing, and finally getting off the bier altogether and mounting triumphantly into the air. Another representation of the resurrection of Osiris shows him with stalks of corn springing from his corpse, whence it is surmised that Osiris, like Demeter and many another divine person of the ancient mythólogies, was supposed to be responsible in some way for the sprouting of the corn and its growth to harvest.

Certain it is that the Egyptians put their trust in Osiris as one who could raise them from the dead and take them with him into his heavenly palace, there to live in everlasting joy. Mummies have been discovered with pictures of Osiris painted on the breast, and many contain little figures of Osiris. On occasion, it seems, grains of corn and barley were placed with the corpse, and these sprang up and flourished for a short time. It would be difficult to think of a more beautiful expression of a beautiful hope.

Good Cheer at Martinmas

November 11 is for us " Armistice Day," commemorating the " cease fire " of the Great War in 1918—at the eleventh hour of the eleventh day of the eleventh month; and also the end of the Second World War in 1945. But for many hundreds of years it has been kept up by English country-folk as the festival of Martinmas—St. Martin's Mass.

Martin was the son of a Roman officer in Hungary, and was born about A.D. 316 and died in 399. Rather reluctantly, he became a soldier, but after several years' service retired from the world to become a hermit. Then in 374 he was appointed Bishop of Tours, in France, and proved a very active bishop. All the pagan temples that remained in his diocese he closed or converted into Christian churches. He was also very charitable, and a famous legend says that once, when still a soldier, he divided his cloak with a poor naked beggar whom he found shivering with cold at the gate of Amiens. (This cloak was believed to have been miraculously preserved, and the French kings used to have it carried in front of the army when they went out to battle, confident that it would bring certain victory. The room in which the *cappa* or cloak of St. Martin was kept acquired the name of *chapelle*, whence our word " chapel.")

Martinmas came at the time of the year when cattle used to be slaughtered and salted down for winter fare (the old Anglo-Saxon name for the month was Blotmonath, i.e. blood month, for this reason), when geese were still in the prime of condition, and the new wine was drawn from the barrel and tasted to see how good it was. Hence it is not surprising that the festival became indeed a feast-day, when the country people ate their fill and drank quite as much as was good for them, since they knew full well that winter was approaching fast, when food would be not too plentiful and quite lacking in variety. This state of affairs has really nothing to do with the soldier-saint, and there can be no doubt that St. Martin's name has been given to what was originally a pagan celebration of good cheer.

DECEMBER

CHRISTMAS comes but once a year—unfortunately, shall we say?—but in olden days the festivities were not crammed into just the two days of Christmas Eve and Christmas Day.

In some places in England, cathedral cities for the most part, a beginning was made on St. Nicholas's Day, December 6, with the election of the " Boy Bishop "—or *Episcopus puerorum*, if you prefer the Latin. One of the choirboys was chosen by his companions to act the part, and he was entitled to wear bishop's robes and to go in procession just as the real bishop would do. If he died during his term of office—which was until Childermas or Holy Innocents' Day, the day (December 28) commemorating the massacre of the infants of Bethlehem by King Herod's orders, as told in the second chapter of St. Matthew's Gospel—he was given the funeral honours of a bishop and had a monument erected to his memory; in Salisbury Cathedral there is a monument which is popularly supposed to represent a Boy Bishop in his robes. The procession through the city streets was very much to the taste of the citizens, who made it the occasion of much horseplay. As late as 1556 the Boy Bishop went in procession through the heart of London on his way to St. Paul's Cathedral, where he preached a sermon. The better sort of citizens, however, looked with disapproval on the custom as tending to be a mockery of sacred things, and when the Reformation was firmly established under Queen Elizabeth there was an end to Boy Bishops and their junketings.

Good Saint Nicholas

Why the election took place on St. Nicholas's Day is not at all clear. Not very much is known about this saint, but he was archbishop of a city in Asia Minor and became not only "Santa Claus" but also the patron saint of Russia, and was regarded as the special protector of young unmarried girls, children, and sailors. Scholars too were under his guardianship. Many legends are told about him. One says that he was a very wealthy man who loved to do good by stealth, and that he once gave three bags of gold to an impoverished nobleman who was unable to provide marriage-portions for his three daughters, so that they were likely to have to lead a miserable and evil life. (The three golden balls that are the pawnbroker's sign are supposed by some to be derived from this timely present.) Probably it was this story that led to the habit of the older members of a family placing sweets and suchlike small gifts in the shoes of the youngsters on the eve of St. Nicholas' Day; when the presents were discovered in the morning, the boys and girls were told that they were due to "good St. Nicholas." In convents the young nuns used to place a pair of silk stockings outside the door of the Mother Abbess.

Another story is that a gentleman once told his three sons to call on Archbishop Nicholas on their way to boarding-school at Athens. At the inn at which they stopped one night they were murdered by wicked men, and their bodies, cut up into pieces, were put in a pickling-tub with some pork. But the Archbishop was told of the horrid deed in a dream, went to the inn, and forced the landlord to confess.

Then the saint made the sign of the Cross over the tub, and immediately the three boys became whole and alive again. This is why in many pictures of St. Nicholas he is shown standing in fine bishop's vestments beside a tub containing three naked boys.

THE LORD OF MISRULE
(*from an old print*)

Master of Merry Disports

Now let us make the better acquaintance of the Lord of Misrule. As one old chronicler explains,

in the feast of Christmas, there was in the King's house, wheresoever he lodged, a Lord of Misrule, or Master of Merry Disports, and the like had ye in the house of every nobleman of honour or good worship, were he spiritual or temporal. . . . These "lords," beginning their rule at Allhallows Eve, continued the same till the morrow after the Feast of the Purification (of the Blessed Virgin Mary) commonly called Candlemas Day, in which space there were fine and subtle disguisings, masks, and mummeries, with playing at cards for counters, nails and points, in every house, more for pastime than for gain.

In Scotland they used to elect an " Abbot of Unreason," whose character and functions were very much the same as those of the Lord of Misrule; one is described by Scott in *The Abbot*:

A stout-made, undersized fellow, whose thick squab form had been rendered grotesque by a supplemental paunch, well stuffed. He wore a mitre of leather, with the front like a grenadier's cap, adorned with mock embroidery and trinkets of tin. This surmounted a visage the nose of which was the most prominent feature. . . . His robe was of buckram, and his cope of canvas, curiously painted, and cut into open work. On one shoulder was fixed the painted figure of an owl; and he bore in the right hand his pastoral staff, and in the left a small mirror. . . .

Such was " the Venerable Father Howleglas, the learned Monk of Misrule, and the Right Reverend Abbot of Unreason "; and as such he played a conspicuous part for many a year in revels which later ages came to look upon as deplorable lapses into irreverence.

The days pass, and now it is Christmas Eve. Scott, in *Marmion*, has some lines of vivid description of the ancient celebrations.

Heap on more wood !—the wind is chill:
But let it whistle as it will,
We'll keep our Christmas merry still.
Each age has deem'd the new-born year
The fittest time for festal cheer:
Even heathen yet, the savage Dane
At Iol more deep the mead did drain;
High on the beach his galleys drew,
And feasted all his pirate crew;

Then in his low and pine-built hall,
Where shields and axes deck'd the wall,
They gorged upon the half-dress'd steer;
Caroused in seas of sable beer;
While round, in brutal jest, were thrown
The half-gnaw'd rib, and marrow-bone,
Or listen'd all, in grim delight,
While scalds yell'd out the joys of fight.
Then forth, in frenzy, would they hie,
While wildly-loose their red locks fly,
And dancing round the blazing pile,
They make such barbarous mirth the while,
As best might to the mind recall
The boisterous joys of Odin's hall.

Many centuries later, " our Christian sires of old
. . . gave honour to the holy night."

On Christmas eve the bells were rung;
On Christmas eve the mass was sung . . .

The damsel " donn'd her kirtle sheen," the merry-
men went out into the wood to gather mistletoe, the
Baron's hall was opened wide to vassal, tenant, serf,
and all.

The heir, with roses in his shoes,
That night might village partner choose;
The Lord, underogating, share
The vulgar game of " post and pair."
All hail'd, with uncontroll'd delight,
And general voice, the happy night,
That to the cottage, as the crown,
Brought tidings of salvation down. . . .

Those were the days of the wassail bowl, the huge
sirloin of beef, when " plumb-porridge stood, and
Christmas pye," when " came the merry maskers in,
And carols roar'd with blithesome din. . . ."

England was merry England, when
Old Christmas brought his sports again.

English literature is filled with similar accounts of the "good old English Christmas," so that the remark one sometimes hears, that "Dickens invented Christmas," is absurdly untrue. What Dickens did do, perhaps, was to transform the season of good cheer—too much good cheer, very often!—into one of kindly remembrance, of family reunions, of love and charity. Many a page he devoted to a description of Christmas. Who that has ever read *Pickwick Papers* will forget the festivities at Dingley Dell? Who has not been moved by the sentiment of *The Christmas Carol*?

Christmas at Bracebridge Hall

But one of the best descriptions of the old-time Christmas such as our great-grandfathers enjoyed is given by the American writer, Washington Irving, who came to England rather more than a century ago. In the pages of his *Sketchbook* we may be whirled along the Yorkshire roads in a stage-coach that is crowded with passengers going home for Christmas and is loaded with hampers of game and baskets and boxes of good Christmas fare. We stand at his elbow when he meets his old friend Frank Bracebridge, and gladly accompany him when he accepts the invitation to Bracebridge Hall. There we join the huge family circle, of relatives and friends and servants; warm our hands at the grate where burns the massive Yule Log; sit down to a supper of frumenty—a dish made of wheat cakes boiled in milk, with rich spices added—and mince-pies; and then share in the dance or revels in the servants' hall, where are kept up "the old games of hoodman blind, shoe the wild mare, hot cockles, steal the white loaf, bob apples, and snap dragon," and perhaps take an interest in " the mistletoe, with its white berries, hung up, to the imminent peril of all the pretty housemaids." (The mistletoe, says Irving for the benefit of his American readers, " is still hung up in farmhouses and kitchens at Christmas, and the young men have the privilege of kissing the girls under it, plucking each time a berry from the bough. When the berries are all plucked, the privilege ceases.") Then Christmas morning, and after a short service in the chapel, we breakfast on cold meats, wine, and ale, and walk across the park to the village church for morning service. There we find the old clergyman reproving the sexton for including among the decorations that " unholy plant " the mistletoe, which " had been profaned by having been used by the Druids in their mystic ceremonies."

Returning home, we note the " indications of good cheer reeking from the chimneys of the comfortable farmhouses," and are delighted with the caperings of a band of country lads, in their be-ribboned shirt sleeves, and with greenery in their hats and clubs in their hands, who perform a curious and intricate country dance, which the Squire, our host, says is a lineal descendant of " the sword-dance that was the vogue when the Romans occupied these islands."

Then the dinner, in the great hall, warmed by a crackling fire of logs on the immense hearth. The parson has hardly said grace, when the butler escorts into the hall servants bearing a silver dish on which lies a pig's head, decorated with rosemary, and with a lemon in his mouth. After which we regale ourselves on roast beef and pheasant pie and a heap more of good things, and wind up with a draught from the Wassail Bowl as it is passed from hand to hand. Dinner over and the ladies gone to the drawing-room, the Squire and the parson tell stories of their college days. Then the table is removed, and the hall given up to the merry games of the younger members of the family.

I delight in witnessing the gambols of children [writes Washington Irving], and particularly at this happy holiday season, and could not help stealing out of the drawing-room on hearing one of their peals of laughter. I found them at the game of blind-man's buff. Master Simon, who was the leader of their revels, and seemed on all occasions to fulfil the office of that ancient potentate, the Lord of Misrule, was blinded in the midst of the hall. The little beings were as busy about him as the mock fairies about Falstaff; pinching him, plucking at the skirts of his coat, and tickling him with straws. One fine blue-eyed girl of about thirteen, with her flaxen hair all in beautiful confusion, her frolic face in a glow, her frock half torn off her shoulders, a complete picture of a romp, was the chief tormentor; and, from the slyness with which Master Simon avoided the smaller game, and hemmed this wild little nymph in corners, and obliged her to jump shrieking over chairs, I suspected the rogue of being not a whit more blinded that was convenient.

Well, that is one Christmas of a distant yesterday. Now here is a glimpse at another, and a very different one.

Little Edmund's Plum-Pudding

" On the subject of all feasts of the Church," writes Sir Edmund Gosse in his *Father and Son,**

* Published by William Heinemann Ltd., and by Penguin Books.

a book which gives a remarkably interesting and vivid picture of a childhood in the middle of the Victorian age, "my father held views of an almost grotesque peculiarity." In particular, he looked upon the keeping of Christmas as a hateful act of idolatry. The very name was Popish, he declared, since it means "Christ's Mass," and the antiquity of the so-called feast was a proof of its having been adapted from "horrible heathen rites" and of its being a "soiled relic of the abominable Yule-Tide." So sternly did he denounce the horrors of Christmas that poor little Edmund almost blushed to look at a holly-berry.

When Christmas came round in the year that Mrs. Gosse had died, her husband gave strict orders that there should be no difference in the family meals on that day. He was obeyed, but the servants rebelled in secret and made a small plum-pudding for themselves.

Early in the afternoon [of Christmas Day], the maids—of whom we were now advanced to keeping two—kindly remarked that "the poor dear child ought to have a bit, anyhow," and wheedled me into the kitchen, where I ate a slice of plum-pudding. Shortly, I began to feel that pain inside which in my frail state was inevitable, and my conscience smote me violently. At length I could bear my spiritual anguish no longer, and bursting into the study I called out: "Oh! Papa, Papa, I have eaten of flesh offered to idols!" It took some time, between my sobs, to explain what had happened. Then my Father sternly said: "Where is the accursed thing?" I explained that as much as was left of it was on the kitchen table. He took me by the hand, and ran with me into the midst of the startled servants, seized what remained of the pudding, and with the plate in one hand and me still tight in the other, ran till we reached the dust-heap, where he flung the idolatrous confectionery on to the middle of the ashes, and then raked it deep down into the mass. . . .

That was in 1857, when Edmund Gosse was eight years old; his father, who had such decided views about the wickedness of plum-puddings and other Christmas features, was a prominent member of a small sect of the stricter sort of Christians, who are still among us as the Plymouth Brethren.

Of course, Philip Gosse, the father, was quite right in thinking that Christmas was originally a pagan festival—although probably most of us will think that he was exceedingly wrong-headed in his attitude towards what has been for so many, many centuries essentially a season of good cheer and " good will among men."

The Birthday of the Sun

Christmas is the celebration of the Nativity—of the birth of Jesus Christ in the manger at Bethlehem; and in all the vast literature of the holy scriptures of the world's religions there are no more beautiful pages than those in the Gospels of St. Luke and St. Matthew which tell of the shepherds who watched their flocks by night and heard the angels sing, and of the " Wise Men " who came from afar, guided by a star, and before the homely cradle offered up lordly gifts of gold, frankincense, and myrrh. But no one knows for certain the year of the Nativity, or the month or the day. In the early days of Christianity some Christians kept Christmas on January 1 and some on January 6; others celebrated it on March 29, the time of the Jewish Passover, and yet others postponed it until September 29. But in the old Roman Empire December 25 was the winter solstice and was regarded as the birthday of the Sun, since on or about that day the days begin to get longer and the Sun seems to get more powerful after its winter decline. The ancient Egyptians, we are told, used to represent the new-born Sun by the image of an infant, which on his birthday they brought forth from the temples and exposed for all to see, saying at the same time, " The Virgin "—that is Isis, the " Queen of Heaven "—" has brought forth! The light is waxing! " Mithra, the Sun-God of the ancient Persians, was supposed to have been born on December 25 ; so, too, according to some, was Buddha, and likewise Freya, one of the old Scandinavian gods. The Druids made the day their annual fire-festival.

Saturnalian Revels in Old Rome

More important still, the ancient Romans used to celebrate on December 19 to 24 the great festival of the Saturnalia, in honour of the god Saturn, which was marked by much merry-making. During this festival the slaves were allowed to enjoy complete freedom of speech and behaviour, and it is said that their masters waited on them as servants. Everyone feasted and rejoiced ; all work was suspended ; the houses were decorated with laurels and evergreens ; presents were given by parents, children, friends and neighbours ; and all sorts of games and amusements were indulged in by one and all. There can be no doubt that our Christmas customs of today are derived very largely from the Roman Saturnalia ; and, indeed, the early Christian missionaries, coming in the main from Rome and lands included in the Roman Empire, thought it a very sensible thing to

Christianize, as it were, the old heathen festival with which their converts were so well acquainted and which they loved too well to abandon altogether.

Other elements in the Christmas programme may be drawn from sources nearer home.

The mistletoe, for instance, played a great part in the worship of the Druids, the priests of the ancient Britons. Apparently it was regarded as a cure for barrenness of humans and animals, and a safeguard against poison. The white-robed Druids used to cut the mistletoe-bough from an oak-tree with a golden sickle, and drop it carefully into a white cloth held below. The mistletoe thus gathered was divided into portions and distributed among the people, who hung it up near the entrances to their huts, as a safeguard against the anger of the gods.

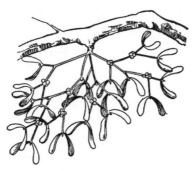

A MISTLETOE-BOUGH

The Sad Story of Balder

The Scandinavians—including the Danes who invaded England in such strength a thousand or so years ago, and settled in many of the northern and midland and eastern shires—also highly revered the mistletoe-bough. They associated it with Balder, the god of poetry and eloquence and the best of the divinities of the old Norse pantheon.

There came a time, runs the legend, when this young and beautiful god had a foreboding of his death. He told his mother, Frigga, and she took counsel with the other gods how this dire happening might be prevented. Then she obtained a promise from fire and water, iron and every other metal, earth and stones, trees, poisons, sickness of every kind, birds and beasts and plants—indeed, from everybody and everything—that never would they do anything to hurt Balder. So the gods used to amuse themselves by throwing things at Balder, and roared with delight when they failed to hit him, or if they did hit him, inflicted not the least injury. Balder enjoyed the rough sport as much as anybody.

But there was among the divine host one Loki, who delighted in making mischief. So one day he disguised himself as an old woman, and inquired of Frigga if it were indeed the case that *everything* had sworn never to hurt Balder? Frigga, in a very unwise burst of confidence, admitted that in her search she had forgotten to demand the oath from the mistletoe; it seemed to be too young to swear, she said. Whereupon Loki went away, picked a mistletoe-bough and put it in the hands of the blind god Höd or Hother; " See if you can hit Balder," he urged him. Höd, anxious to join in the fun, flung the bough as Loki directed his arm, and Balder was pierced through and through by the bough, and fell down dead. Whereupon his body was burnt on the funeral pyre, and all the gods mourned the passing of the brightest and best among them.

Burning the Yule-log

The Yule-log, too, had mystic associations in the
religion of the old Norsemen.   At the winter solstice,
we learn, they used to kindle huge bonfires in honour

BRINGING HOME THE YULE-LOG
(*from an old print*)

of the great god Thor.   Possibly it was a kind of
Sun-worship, or the winter equivalent of the bonfires of spring : a magical rite intended to encourage
and assist the Sun in that time of his annual career
when he was obviously feeling very " low."   In
England, and in many parts of Germany and France
and other countries, the Yule-log used to be cut
with care, dragged home, and placed on the hearth

with loud rejoicings. When it was all burnt, its ashes were carefully collected, either (as in some places) to be strewn on the fields as a fertilizer on every night up to Twelfth Night, or (as in others) to be kept as a charm and useful medicine. French peasants used to believe that if the ashes were kept under the bed, they would protect the house against thunder and lightning, as well as preventing chilblains on the heels all the winter through. Why, they were even capable of keeping bugs away !

Herrick has some lines about the Yule-Log—

> Come bring with a noise
> My merry, merry boys,
> The Christmas log to the firing . . .
> With the last year's brand
> Light the new block—

which allude to another old practice, that of keeping a half-consumed piece of the old log with which to light the new one the following Christmas. This was considered to be of very high importance, whether, as some writers say, because it constituted a kind of fire-insurance ; or whether, which seems more likely, it was the symbol of the undying vigour of the Sun.

Thus we see that two popular observances of the old-time Christmas—the hanging up of the mistletoe, and the burning of the Yule-log—are of definitely pagan origin. So true is it, as Robert Chambers says, that " to investigate the origin of many of our Christmas customs, it becomes necessary to wander far back into the regions of past time, long ere Julius Caesar had set his foot on our shores, or St.

Augustine preached the doctrines of Christianity to the men of Kent."

The Christmas Tree is said to have been unknown in England until the middle of the last century, when Prince Albert introduced it from Germany—

CAROL SINGERS ON CHRISTMAS MORNING
(*from an old print*)

where it has been part of the Christmas proceedings for many centuries—to amuse the young princes and princesses at Windsor. Christmas cards are a modern invention: the first was made in 1846. Christmas carols seem to be almost as old as Christianity itself; the first carols, we are assured, were those the angels sang on the night Jesus was born. As Milton says, in *Paradise Lost*:

His place of birth a solemn Angel tells
To simple shepherds, keeping watch by night;
They gladly thither haste, and by a choir
Of squadron'd Angels hear his carol sung.

The good old Vicar of Wakefield in Goldsmith's novel praised his parishioners for keeping up the Christmas Carol; perhaps they sang, as we sing today, " God rest you merry, gentlemen," or " I saw three ships come sailing in, On Christmas-day, on Christmas-day."

Christmas decorations of holly and laurel and ivy derive from the Roman Saturnalia and from the customs of the ancient Druids. In present-day England all Christmas greenery must be taken down by Twelfth Night, but in older times it was believed that Candlemas Day (February 2) was the limit. Sang Herrick: " Down with the rosemary, down with the holly, ivy, all . . .

That so the superstitious find
No one least branch there left behind;
For look, how many leaves there be
Neglected there, maids trust to me,
So many goblins you shall see.

Here perhaps we may note an old-time custom in Oxfordshire. It was the custom of maidservants to ask a man for ivy to decorate the house; if he refused, or did not bring enough, they stole a pair of his breeches and nailed them on a gate in the yard or in the road. Elsewhere the penalty for his refusal or neglect was a disdainful toss of the head when he tried to snatch a kiss from a good-looking girl underneath the mistletoe.

Then there is Christmas fare. Here again there

is to be traced the direct descent from the banquet-
ings of the Saturnalia and the rude guzzlings of the
Scandinavian chieftains in their halls. The boar's
head is a thing of the past, and nowadays we do not
think of the peacock as specially appropriate for
Christmas dinner. Geese and fowls and turkeys—
these our ancestors fancied just as much as we do.
Mince-pies have been popular for at least four
hundred years, and plum-puddings are perhaps as
old. As for drinking, there we are at a disadvantage
as compared with our ancestors, who knew nothing
of tea and coffee, but drank strong ale at breakfast,
dinner, and supper, and at all times in between.

The Christmas pantomime is another ancient
custom, deriving from the drama of old Rome and
Greece. At the Saturnalia the practice of mas-
querading, when men donned women's masks and
vice versa, was very popular ; so popular, indeed,
that the Christian clergy found it impossible to
suppress it. Accordingly they transformed it, as they
transformed so many other customs. Instead of
heathen revels there were now miracle- and mystery-
plays, that is, dramatic representations of incidents
in the lives of the saints and of the Bible respectively.
For many centuries such religious plays were very
popular, not only at Christmas but also at other
great seasons of the Church's year, and often the
clergy took parts. After the Reformation these
plays were performed by " mummers," and they
seem to have been the ancestors of the charades and
other " dressing-up " at our Christmas parties. In
Thomas Hardy's *The Return of the Native* * there is

* Published by Macmillan & Co. Ltd.

CHRISTMAS IN OLD ENGLAND—BRINGING IN THE BOAR'S HEAD
(From the illustration by R. Seymour in T. K. Hervey's *Book of Christmas*, 1837)

an account of a mummers' performance in a Dorset village, when they acted " the well-known play of *St. George.*" " Make room, make room, my gallant boys," roared Father Christmas—what *he* was doing there is not very clear—" and give us space to rhyme "; and then Saint George himself enters with a magnificent flourish :

Here come I, Saint George, the valiant man,
With naked sword and spear in hand,
Who fought the dragon and brought him to the slaughter
And by this won fair Sabra, the King of Egypt's daughter. . . .

As for Boxing Day, the day after Christmas Day, when " Christmas-boxes " are given, here again there is a reminder of the old Roman custom of giving and receiving presents during the Saturnalia.

Whipping the Innocents

Three days after Christmas is the day which in the Church calendar is called Innocents' Day, or Childermas. Years ago the day used to be considered very unlucky, and so there was no question of getting married upon it, or of embarking upon any important business. In Cornwall, we are assured, housewives used to refrain from scrubbing on Innocents' Day ; though whether they expected that someone would enter forthwith with dirty feet or for whatever other reason is not clear. Certainly it was an unlucky day for children—at least in those homes where, as an old writer puts it, the custom was " to whip up the children upon Innocents' Day morning, that the memorie of Herod's murder of the Innocents might stick the closer, and in a moderate proportion to act over the crueltie again in kinde." But very often the youngsters used to take a careful note of the calendar, and on the morning of December 28 got up particularly early, and skipped out of doors to play.

Hogmanay at Year's End

So we come to the last day of the year. It is not made much of in England, but in Scotland it is what Christmas is with the " Sassenachs." The old name for the festival is Hogmanay, and the etymologists have had a fine time of it trying to determine this strange word's origin. One theory is that it comes from the Greek words for " holy month." Another, referring to an old song in which the rollicking chorus is " Hogmanay, trollolay ! " says it is a corruption of the French *Homme est né—Trois Rois là* ("A man is born—i.e. Christ—Three Kings are there"); this seems altogether too fanciful. More plausible is the suggestion that it comes from Hog-night, the old Scandinavian name for the night preceding the feast of Yule, when the animals were slaughtered for Christmas fare, *hogg* signifying " to kill." Perhaps the most likely derivation is from the Old French *aguilanneuf*, which is a running together of the words for " To the mistletoe ! the New Year ! "

Be that as it may, the last day of the year is one of merry-making among the Scots, wherever they may be. In some parts the children still go round the town singing the songs associated from time immemorial with this season of the year. One of these runs :

Get up, goodwife, and shake your feathers,
And dinna think that we are beggars ;
For we are bairns come out to play,
Get up and gie us our hogmanay.

What they hope to get, as they call at house after house on their route, is a section of oatcake which some housewives, knowing the old-time custom, have baked in readiness.

In the West of England the country people on New Year's Eve go round the orchards and wassail the apple-trees. Solemn incantations are spoken, guns are fired into the air to scare away evil spirits, and pieces of toast soaked in cider are hung on the trees to induce the birds to spare the fruit when it comes. Beyond a doubt such customs are pagan survivals.

A practice has grown up in England of holding a " watchnight service " in church at eleven o'clock on December 31 ; it serves as a solemn reminder of the passing of time, with its opportunities for doing good, and also for making resolutions that the New Year shall be a better one in every sense than the one that is fast slipping into history. Such services were originally held by the Methodists in the Wesleys' day, in the eighteenth century, but they have now spread to many other Christian bodies.

Very different are the convivial scenes that are to be witnessed outside St. Paul's Cathedral in London and similarly important and central buildings elsewhere, when the crowds make merry in a boisterous fashion and usually show signs of having taken more than a " wee drappie " of strong drink. Pleasanter far is the sound of the ships' sirens in the river as midnight strikes, and of the whistles blown by the engine-drivers as the trains go past.

But surely the most appropriate sound of all is that of the church bells, pealing in the night. At first they seem to have a touch of sadness : one is reminded of those who have left us in the year that has gone, of the vacant chairs of those we have loved and lost. One thinks of all that we might have done, and did not do ; of how another year of our allotted span has gone.

But then the bells take on a gladder note, and with heartfelt sincerity we echo the wish that Tennyson expressed so finely in his poem *In Memoriam*:

> Ring out the old, ring in the new,
>   Ring, happy bells, across the snow :
>   The year is going, let him go ;
> Ring out the false, ring in the true.

INDEX

205